BLACK MAN
ON THE
TITANIC

Also by Serge Bilé

Noirs dans les camps nazis

La légende du sexe surdimensionné des Noirs

Sur le dos des hippopotames

Tiwa et la pierre miroir

Quand les Noirs avaient des esclaves blancs

*Le miracle oublié: chronique des apparitions de la Vierge Marie
en Martinique*

*Et si Dieu n'aimait pas les Noirs? Enquête sur le racisme aujourd'hui
au Vatican*

*Au secours, le prof est noir! Enquête sur le racisme dans l'Éducation
nationale* (with Mathieu Méranville)

Blanchissez-moi tous ces nègres

*Sombres Bourreaux: collabos africains, antillais, guyanais,
réunionnais et noirs américains, dans la Deuxième Guerre mondiale*

La Mauresse de Moret: La religieuse au sang bleu

Singe, les dangers de la bananisation des esprits (with Audifac Ignace)

BLACK MAN
ON THE
TITANIC

The Story of Joseph Laroche

SERGE BILÉ

Mango Publishing
CORAL GABLES, FL

Published by Mango Publishing Group, a division of Mango Media Inc.

Cover Design: Morgane Leoni
Layout & Design: Morgane Leoni

For permission requests, please contact the publisher at:
Mango Publishing Group
2850 S Douglas Road, 2nd Floor
Coral Gables, FL 33134 USA
info@mango.bz

For special orders, quantity sales, course adoptions and corporate sales, please email the publisher at sales@mango.bz. For trade and wholesale sales, please contact Ingram Publisher Services at customer.service@ingramcontent.com or +1.800.509.4887.

Black Man on the Titanic: The Story of Joseph Laroche

Library of Congress Cataloging-in-Publication number: 2019932090
ISBN: (print) 978-1-63353-958-7, (ebook) 978-1-63353-959-4
BISAC category code HIS056000—HISTORY / African American

Translated from French by: Logan Masterworks, Miami, FL

Printed in the United States of America

Contents

Preface

The sinking of the *Titanic* in April 1912 generated within a century a multitude of books, films, and video games. Each of these honed in on the drama of the accident in all its forms, focusing mostly on the personality and the psychology of many of the passengers. But the tragic story of Joseph Philippe Lemercier Laroche has been largely excluded from history.

At a time of heightened racial imbalance and hostility, a Black man from Haiti boarded the *RMS Titanic*—not as a crew member, but as a paying passenger: one of the few Black passengers on board the famous ship. Raised in a world of stultifying expectations about race, Joseph Laroche was educated in France, where he found professional successes and contributed to the construction of the Parisian railway. What do we know about Laroche, a direct relative of Jean-Jacques Dessalines, the first ruler of independent Haiti? How was his childhood in Cap-Haïtien, and how did he come to travel to Beauvais, Lille, and Paris? Why did he give up first-class tickets for the luxury ship *La France* to board the *Titanic* with his wife and two daughters? Where was he going—and why?

That is the story I tell: the true story of one black man whose triumphs were shadowed by prejudice, social expectations, and tragedy, but also the remarkable story of a time period. As I delve into black history and the singular bonds between the United States and the Antilles, this is definitely not "just another book about the Titanic." While *The Black Man on the Titanic* covers the tragedy, offering a new approach to a slice of history that still fascinates millions, it also presents little-known aspects of the African American and Caribbean experience.

In order to properly honor Joseph Laroche's story, I used a narrative style throughout much of this book, combining source material from letters, interviews, newspapers, and archives to create a more engaging narrative.

Because I relied on testimonials and secondary sources and, as we all know, human memory is deeply flawed, some events have been compressed and some conversations and inner dialogue have been recreated in varying degrees. I retold them in a way that evokes the feeling and meaning of what was said and, in all instances, the essence of the dialogue (both internal and external) is accurate. *Any mistakes are mine.*

I would like to thank the descendants of the family portrayed in this book for the privilege of interviewing them, particularly Christina Schutt, the great-grandniece of Joseph Laroche, who not only provided letters and other written materials, but also shared her family's oral history.

Thank you to Georges Michel, Christian Boutillier, and Bruno Rousseau. All the interviewees are good, hard-working people who helped with my research immensely. Christian Boutillier shared with me a file that documented everyday life at École du Saint-Esprit in Beauvais, which allowed me to recreate the time Joseph Laroche spent at the school, although nothing in the file directly referred to Laroche himself. Bruno Rousseau, who attended the same Jesuit school I did, forty years ago in France, helped me remember the details of boarding school life: the masses, the studies, the games... Our conversations revived my own memories and helped me walk in Joseph Laroche's shoes.

I was given access to a variety of written sources thanks to François Codet of the French Titanic Society, Father Roger Tabard of the Congregation of the Holy Spirit, and Myriam Sylvain, who generously introduced me to Gaétan Mentor from the Haitian Historical Society.

The French Titanic Society gave me access to its archives, where I found various newspaper articles from France and Canada focused on the tragedy experienced by the family of Joseph Laroche.

Father Roger Tabard allowed me to consult the archives of Congrégation du Saint-Esprit and gather the information needed to write about the functioning of the school attended by Joseph Laroche: the roles of the priests, of the administration, of the teachers. I didn't find much about Joseph Laroche himself, besides the eulogy I mention in the book, but the wealth of information allowed for a more detailed account.

While writing *The Black Man on the Titanic,* I have occasionally added my personal spin to the story, mostly to fill in gaps as best I could, but I have done my best to make it a truthful story.

SERGE BILÉ

I. The New York Express

Cherbourg[1], April 19, 1996. An elderly woman is clutching a small black purse in her lap. The purse is black, as is the long coat she is wearing this afternoon. Black is appropriate, because she is still in mourning, eighty-four years after the sinking of the *Titanic*. Sitting on an iron chair, alone, under the gaze of a sympathetic crowd, she has just unveiled a plaque in memory of the 281 passengers who boarded the famous ocean liner during its stopover in Normandy. The plaque, covered with a blue cloth, is affixed to a headstone made of granite and shaped like a menhir, pointing toward the sky.

Not a word, not a movement. The woman is silent. She seems frozen, both submerged and crushed by emotion. Her face is contorted, but no tears stream down her cheeks. Her lips shape into a scream, but no sound escapes.

Eighty-four years ago, Louise Laroche[2] was on this same dock, at Ancien-Arsenal.

This is where passengers boarded the two ferries that took them to the *Titanic*, a colossal ship anchored off the coast, outside the harbor. Two strong arms had lifted her aboard. It should have been the beginning of an unforgettable voyage, the trip of a lifetime.

Eighty-four years later, her muscles bent by age and hardship, Louise Laroche is looking everywhere, on the dock, on the ocean, among the people, searching for the slightest memory, but to no avail. She cannot remember anything.

How could it be otherwise? She was not even two years old when it all happened. And nothing is the same. The dock itself has been renamed after Lawton-Collins[3], an American general. Lawton-Collins, they told her, was in charge of the Seventh Army Corps that landed on June 6, 1944, not far away, on Utah Beach. He and his men freed Cherbourg.

Cherbourg

The second largest man-made harbor in the world at the time, Cherbourg-Octeville was the first stop on the *Titanic*'s maiden voyage. *Titanic* arrived in Cherbourg in the late afternoon. Two tenders, *Nomadic* and *Traffic*, transported 281 passengers from the dock to the fated liner which was moored in Cherbourg's harbor. The dock was later renamed after an American General by the name of Lawton-Collins whose men freed Cherbourg during World War II. In Cherbourg, a plaque was unveiled by Louise Laroche in memory of the passengers who'd boarded the RSM *Titanic.*

Yes, everything has changed since the *Titanic* catastrophe. There were other sinkings: the two World Wars sank the "civilized world" big-time, plunging millions of families into mourning. The Cherbourg port, a strategic target, was bombed and destroyed. Since then, of course, it has been rebuilt, but it's nothing like it was before.

The small ferry terminal that, in the old days, used to welcome the eager passengers of the arriving and departing liners has become a huge "passenger terminal" for new cruise travelers. What is left of it, anyway. The magic and glamour of those bygone years are no more. Gone are the beautiful times of the *"transats,"* those transatlantic steamers.

To Louise, it is a strange moment. She has been digging in the most hidden corners of her mind, but her widely-praised "faithful memory" fails her. She does not remember anything, absolutely anything, other than this haunting date that brought her here today in Cherbourg.

■ ■ ■

Young Simonne Laroche had gotten up at dawn. She'd washed up and brushed her teeth in a rush and put on festive clothes. She was excited at the idea of traveling from Paris in a luxurious train and, once in Cherbourg, boarding the *Titanic,* the most beautiful liner in the world.

After breakfast, her family hired not one but two taxicabs that morning, two Renault AG1s[4] that started with crank handles. Sitting on a trunk with leather cushions, the driver maneuvered a wooden steering wheel and used two long levers at his lower right to change speeds. After the luggage had been evenly distributed in the trunks and on the fold-up seats of the passenger cabin, three-year-old Simone climbed into the first taxi with her father, Joseph. She settled herself in the back seat so she would not miss a thing; she watched the fabulous spectacle from the window, raving in each instant over the dance of the cars and the carriages, pulled by robust horses. In the second vehicle, her mother Juliette held on to Simone's younger sister, twenty-one-month-old Louise.

Renault AG1s

To get from Paris to Cherbourg-Octeville, the Laroche family hired two Renault AG1s that started with crank handles. The AG1 (Taxi de la Marne) was the first car produced after Marcel Renault's death in 1903. It used a taximeter, a relatively new invention that automatically calculated how much the passenger had to pay. According to the *Renaud Classic* website, "Taxi service provided valuable exposure for the Renault name and brought it recognition beyond France. In 1907, Renault sold 1,100 units in London." The name Taxi de la Marne was not used until the outbreak of World War I, when 1,300 taxis were requisitioned by the French Army to transport 6,000 soldiers from Paris to the First Battle of the Marne in early September 1914.

April 10, 1912, was a beautiful, sunny day. A day made for traveling. For Simone, who was in raptures over everything, it felt like Christmas in April. The trip from Paris had felt like an expedition. Since the Saint-Lazare train station was only a dozen kilometers from Villejuif[5], where the family lived, it took them less than an hour to get there. Simone was disappointed: the spectacle had been too short.

She was in such a hurry to climb aboard the *Titanic* that she rushed ahead of the group. Until a voice called to her: "*Simone, rété la!*" It was her father, urging her to stay with him. Whenever Joseph Laroche scolded Simone, he did so in Creole[6]. He raised his voice with authority, not anger. Simone did not always know what the Creole words meant, but she understood their urgency and obeyed immediately and without fear.

Louise was not scared of Joseph Laroche either. On the contrary. She melted into her mustached father's smiles and hugs. On that day, however, she was getting impatient in the stroller. She wanted to get out. She would have loved to walk on the dock like her sister. She stomped. She twisted and turned. "Daddy! Daddy, boat! Daddy, get down! Daddy, boat!" Louise exclaimed, a typical toddler begging to explore the ship. She loved being taken around like this. She showed it with a blissful smile that disappeared as soon as the stroller ride was over. The baby carriage was Louise's "little car," joked her mother, who later told her what little she could remember about that time.

Three months earlier, when her father had announced his decision to return to the faraway country of his birth, his wife and children in tow, Simone had happily welcomed the news. Not that she wanted to flee France, but she was tired of the never-ending winter. She found the cold deceptive. On the first day of April, for instance, "mild weather" had been forecast. Yet, the thermometer had bottomed out; it had snowed in Paris in the wee hours of the morning and again between ten and eleven o'clock. Simone had hated it. She loved the idea of an escape: to leave Villejuif for Cherbourg, then New York, and finally the sunny Caribbean.

By April 10, 1912, however, the milder weather was back. There were sure signs of spring, and the temperature had reached 77 degrees Fahrenheit on the banks of the Seine. Simone felt revived. It might have been worth staying, but it was too late. The two Renault AG1s had reached their destination and her father was paying the fare. Now that it was time to take the plunge and leave France for good, Simone was hesitant. She thought about her grandfather, who was staying home alone. She wondered if she would ever see him again.

However, Simone's pout disappeared when, at the center of the Cour de Rome, she spotted Monsieur Renard, a friend of her parents, who sometimes visited their home. He had come to bid them farewell, holding two beautiful balloons. At the sight of the balloon that was intended for her, Louise started kicking and clapping vigorously. She grabbed the gift and began shaking it in all directions, giggling. But, in her excitement, she let go of the string and burst into tears when the balloon flew away. Monsieur Renard comforted her and immediately went to buy her another one.

As Monsieur Renard and the Laroches entered the Saint-Lazare station, the rush of people swallowed them. The children were in awe of the crowded Café Terminus, of the bustling platforms, of the railway men in their uniforms and the porters weighed down by suitcases. Travelers hurried to get to their cars, the women in beautiful outfits and the men with elegant top hats.

"Mom, look!" Simone said, pointing at the building's brilliant metal frame and glass roof. She took two steps forward, two more back, stopped, and then lifted her head again as a ray of sun filled the concourse, accentuating the vastness of the place.

"*Simone, rété la!*" her father called when Simone let go of her mother's hand and walked away, as she did every time something intriguing or enthralling captivated her. She could not help it: the wonders of the world were like magnets. She could not resist them! To Simone, the sights at the Saint-Lazare station were even more beautiful than the view she'd admired from the Renault AG1 taxi. She watched a locomotive chug away as big smoke clouds puffed to the sky.

Two special trains had been arranged for the *Titanic*. The first had set forth at 7:45 for Cherbourg, carrying 103 third-class passengers. The second one, scheduled for

9:45, would transport 161 first-class and twenty-seven second-class travelers; the Laroches belonged in that train.

On the platform, Joseph and Juliette exchanged a few more words with Monsieur Renard until, at last, it was time to depart. As the family got into the car, Simone could tell their friend had a heavy heart. The adults, she was sure, pondered one question, although no one dared voice it: When would they see each other again?

The New York Express[7] was a luxury train that included a restaurant and private cabins for the wealthiest, among which was the American magnate John Jacob Astor[8]. Head of a financial empire and a luxury hotel chain, he was traveling with his new spouse Madeleine. In September of the year before, their marriage had shocked America. At seventeen, the young woman was a minor; her husband was forty-eight. In order to escape the scandal, the couple had left for Egypt, and later Europe, along with a valet, a housemaid, a nurse, and a dog. Now that Madeleine was ready to give birth, however, they were back in the United States. In comparison, twenty-three-year-old Joseph and twenty-two-year-old Juliette Laroche lived a simple, private life.

On board the train that reached ninety kilometers an hour, a reasonable speed, the Laroches allowed "Little Simone," as her mother called her, the pleasure of admiring the view. An overly excited Louise had a hard time falling asleep, despite the monotonous turning of the wheels on the railway.

The Laroches did not take long to befriend the other occupants of the cab, Albert and Antonie Mallet[9], a French couple who lived in Canada. Albert Mallet was unpretentious and jovial. He worked for the former mayor of Montreal, Hormidas Laporte[10], who imported alcohol, tea, fruit, and spices from Europe, Asia, and the Caribbean. Mallet was in charge of the cognac orders and often traveled to Paris. He took advantage of the opportunity to bring along his wife and little boy.

John Jacob Astor

John Jacob "Jack" Astor IV (1864–1912) was a wealthy American businessman, a prominent member of the Astor family, and the first multimillionaire in the United States. He traveled with his wife on the opulent New York Express to the *Nomadic* and died in the early hours of the sinking of the *Titanic*. He was the richest passenger aboard and was believed to have been one of the wealthiest men in the world at that time.

Interesting anecdote: A charity once called Astor for a possible contribution, a request he responded to by donating fifty dollars. When being told by a disappointed committee, "Oh, Mr. Astor, your son William gave us a hundred dollars," he replied, "Yes, but you must remember that William has a rich father."

They were on their way back to Quebec with their son André[11], two years old, after a few days vacationing with family in France.

Just like Juliette Laroche, Antonie Mallet, twenty-four, was a stay-at-home mother, content with her life. She found joy in taking care of her son, her husband, and her house. She admitted being envious of Juliette, who proudly flaunted her high hairdo and her round belly.

"When are you due?" Antonie asked.

"Can you believe she's only in her first trimester?" Joseph said, before his wife had a chance to reply.

Albert Mallet laughed heartily, and so did Simone. She was happy. For the first time that day, her father was not frowning. Which one of the four adults had first broken the ice? Who among the Mallets or the Laroches had started the conversation? Was it the husbands between themselves? Was it the wives? After an hour, no one really knew. But that was no longer important. They were friends now, and all delighted by the good company.

Joseph confided to Albert Mallet that he was proud of the fact that one of his children would be born in his home country. The perspective carried some kind of symbolism. What a marvelous way to launch their new life!

To Antonie, Juliette explained that her pregnancy was part of the reason they were traveling on the *Titanic*. The original plan had been to travel later the next year, but when the "unplanned" pregnancy had been revealed a few weeks before, Joseph had decided on an earlier departure, so that the crossing would be less exhausting for his wife.

Otherwise, they would have had to wait another twelve months.

As the train moved toward the unknown and Antonie and Juliette got to know each other, they discovered they both had revised their initial plans.

Both women had first considered embarking on the *France*, another ocean liner of the moment, which followed the same itinerary as the *Titanic*, with a decor just as magical. But when they had learned that children on board were not permitted to eat at the same table as their parents, Antonie and Juliette had changed their minds and finally opted for the *Titanic*.

. . .

On April 19, 1996, as she stands at the commemoration on the dock in Cherbourg, Louise is once again thinking of this twist of fate. Since her father had already purchased the tickets for the *France*, he'd been deeply annoyed by the rule regarding meal times: in the dining room, children occupied an area away from their parents. Thankfully (or so he believed at the time), when he had requested the switch from one liner to the other, the employee at the counter had not given him a hard time.

Louise is overwhelmed by guilt. She's possessed by this irrepressible and fleeting feeling every time she thinks of the *Titanic*, which is often. She is angry at her mother for having told her; she is angry at her father for having changed the reservations. She is angry at herself for being at the root of her family's misfortune, and she is angry at Simone for the same reason.

Louise wishes quite simply that they had never taken the New York Express that day.

. . .

As a cognac merchant, Albert Mallet had the gift of gab and knew how to connect with just about anybody. On the train headed toward Cherbourg, Mallet was happy to break the ice and exchange a few words with Joseph Laroche. He was intrigued by the tall, mustached man who shared his compartment on the New York Express. A black man among all these white people, that was not something one saw every day! As he listened carefully, he quickly understood that his singular fellow traveler was not an American, unlike the other wealthy passengers in first (and second) class. Mallet assumed Laroche to be either West Indian[12] or African.

Portrait of Joseph Laroche

Joseph was not surprised by Mallet's curiosity. He understood why his presence on this train aroused surprise and suspicion. Few black people traveled on liners as magnificent as the *France* and the *Titanic*. And when a West Indian or African did board these superb ships, no one expected him in a second-class car, his entire family in tow, all in their Sunday best.

If Laroche was indeed West Indian, Mallet decided he would talk about rum[13]. Simple. Rum would be a good introduction, as the Frenchman was well-versed in that department. Otherwise, the conversation might stall, as the expert in liquors did not know much about African drinks. In any case, Mallet had a secret weapon: humor.

Albert Mallet struck up most conversations with the same joke, which made him likable from the get-go. The joke itself was not really funny, and people didn't always laugh, but his sense of humor cheered up others and never failed to put a smile on someone else's face. Mallet took a serious tone to explain at once that his life was not worth more than "six cents." The statement usually got a reaction, and his new friend would ask: "Why do you say that?" The reply came in a burst of laughter: "I am worth six cents because I was born on August 6." The connection was established.

Joseph was not surprised by Mallet's curiosity. He understood why his presence on this train aroused surprise and suspicion. Few black people traveled on liners as magnificent as the *France* and the *Titanic*. And when a West Indian or African did board these superb ships, no one expected him in a second-class car, his entire family in tow, all in their Sunday best. A black man would have been a third-class passenger on the 7:45 train, among the Syrian, Slovak, or Italian migrants in search of jobs in America, seeing the *Titanic* as a kind of Trojan horse giving them access to a new world. Joseph was used to people stopping in their tracks to stare at him, as if he were some strange creature. This time, however, he was not annoyed. The interest did not feel morbid, or inappropriate, especially after the very pleasant discussion he had just had with the charming Mallet.

Mallet quickly realized that he was dealing with a gentleman. Not only was Joseph handsome, he also had a stately demeanor that inspired respect. With his elegant, fitted coat and the wide white tie made of fine cloth and wrapped around his collar, the black man looked like a character straight out of an eighteenth-century novel. The effect produced by Joseph was made even more impressive by the contrast that existed between the old-world grandeur he emanated and the youth of his face. The father of two looked like a teenager. No matter what Joseph Laroche did to appear older than his twenty-five years, he could not fool anyone for long. The comments about his youthful looks were unavoidable and often offended him.

What also struck Albert on the train was the chemistry between Joseph and Juliette Laroche. He had noticed how well the two got along and how proud they appeared of each other, which was rather unusual for couples of this kind. Mixed couples, which were not commonplace at the time, were frowned upon. In fact, white women who dared marry black men were considered to have loose morals and were ostracized. Yet, far from hiding their relationship, Juliette Laroche showed her round belly as well as her happiness in sharing her husband's life. The Laroches certainly had not been spared hardship, but nothing had deterred their devotion to each other. On the contrary, their two beautiful daughters were a testimony to the strength of their marriage.

■ ■ ■

The locomotive covered the 350 kilometers between Paris and Cherbourg in less than six hours. Upon arrival, the Laroches had patiently followed the flow, trading their seats on the New York Express for those of the *Nomadic*[14], one of two ferries that transported passengers from the pier to the *Titanic*. The White Star Line[15], the company that owned the *Titanic*, used two shuttles because Cherbourg did not yet have a deep-sea port. The *Nomadic* carried first- and second-class passengers to the ocean liners, while the *Traffic* transported the third class. Passengers on the *Traffic*[16] disembarked first, followed by the *Nomadic* passengers, including the Laroches, who were a good distance away from the rich people of independent means, the bankers and businessmen who constituted the upper crust in this voyage. There was the American Charles Hays[17], president of a railway company, and the British Bruce Ismay[18], president of the White Star Line. For these billionaires, days on the *Titanic* were expected to go by calmly, between luxurious salons and Turkish baths[19], the squash court[20] and the Parisian Café[21], famous for its "lovely veranda bathing in sun, tastefully decorated with French ivy trellis and other climbing plants."

J BRUCE ISMAY

CHAIRMAN, WHITE STAR LINE

J Bruce Ismay survived Titanic's sinking
but never recovered his reputation.
He resigned from IMM and White Star Line
in 1913 though remained chairman and
director of a large number of companies,
including the London and North Western
Railway and the Asiatic Steam Navigation
Company. He spent much of his later years
at his fishing lodge in County Galway.

The women would never wear the same outfit twice. The *Titanic* emulated life in high society, where appearance was everything.

In the evening, the Laroches would either use the elevators or a sumptuous staircase to access the reception room for dinner. Some of the wealthier passengers would be lucky enough to have the honor of sitting at the table of Captain Edward John Smith[22]. This English sexagenarian, affable and imposing, would move back and forth between his distinguished guests and the bridge, where he gave orders and followed the ship's progress.

> **66** You could actually walk miles along the decks and passages covering different ground all the time. I was thoroughly familiar with pretty well every type of ship afloat, but it took me 14 days before I could, with confidence, find my way from one part of that ship to another. **99**
> —Charles Lightoller, Second Officer
> aboard *Titanic*

· · ·

When they boarded the *Titanic*, the Laroches were impressed by the luxury and the immensity of the liner; both surpassed their expectations. Simone saw Joseph open his eyes wide, just like she had a few hours earlier at the Saint-Lazare station. The view in front of them was so staggering that it made their heads spin. The magnificent sights also amazed Juliette, who seemed frozen in place. She bent down toward Simone, who was pointing at the elevator operator in astonishment. As they went up to their cabin, Louise thought she was flying and was gesticulating with happy shouts in her stroller.

**A postage stamp printed in Ireland circa 2012 shows an image
of the RSM *Titanic*.**

Captain Edward John Smith

Edward John Smith (1850–1912) was the captain of the *Titanic* and perished when the ship sank. Smith left school early to join the British Merchant Navy and the Royal Naval Reserve. After earning his master's ticket, he entered the service of the White Star Line. His first command was the SS *Celtic*. He eventually served as commanding officer of numerous White Star Line vessels, including the *Majestic*, which he commanded for nine years. In 1904, Smith became the commodore of the White Star Line, and was responsible for controlling its flagships. He successfully commanded the *Baltic*, *Adriatic*, and the *Olympic*. Smith was posthumously lauded as an example of British stoicism for his conduct aboard the *Titanic*, and his refusal to evacuate as it sank.

"I cannot imagine any condition which would cause a ship to founder. I cannot conceive of any vital disaster happening to this vessel. Modern ship building has gone beyond that."
—Captain Smith, Commander of *Titanic*

"We do not care anything for the heaviest storms in these big ships. It is fog that we fear. The big icebergs that drift into warmer water melt much more rapidly under water than on the surface, and sometimes a sharp, low reef extending two or three hundred feet beneath the sea is formed. If a vessel should run on one of these reefs, half her bottom might be torn away."
—Captain Smith, Commander of *Titanic*

The dining room of the RMS *Titanic*, 1912

The reception room of the RMS *Titanic*, 1912

How could one not be captivated? There was light everywhere, and every detail had been carefully planned to make life on board easy. The second-class passengers had at their disposal a Louis XVI-style smoking room. With the first class, they shared a barbershop, a pool, a library, a promenade deck, and the sought-after Parisian Café. The design was breathtaking, including the most superb woodwork: the sculpted oak paneling, the mahogany-covered walls, and the white wood pillars gleamed with perfection. While many had described the liner as a city, it was in fact a "floating forest."

The Laroches had taken possession of their "apartment," as Joseph called their cabin, with the same joy as the first 944 passengers who, six hours earlier, had boarded the ship in Southampton, the starting point of the *Titanic*'s journey. The cabin was located on rear deck F. It was equipped with very beautiful furniture, a double sink, and a sofa bed, in addition to the bunks.

"This is better than a five-star hotel. This was no rip-off," Juliette exclaimed.

The crossing had cost the entire family a little over forty-one pounds; the ticket, number 2123, delivered by the White Star Line, proved it. Joseph kept it safely in his jacket pocket. To him, second class on the *Titanic* was worth first class on any other liner. There was no comparison anyway with the modest service he'd received, eleven years ago, on the boat that had taken him to France.

" I enjoyed myself as if I were on a summer palace by the seashore surrounded by every comfort. I was up early before breakfast and met the professional racquet player in a half-hours warm-up for a swim in the six-foot-deep tank of saltwater heated to a refreshing temperature. **"**

—Colonel Archibald Gracie, *Titanic* survivor

...

At 8:10 p.m., illuminated by a thousand lights, the *Titanic* left Cherbourg for a last stopover in Queenstown[23], Ireland, where it picked up another one hundred and twenty-three travelers, mainly third-class passengers, some escaping poverty, others in search of adventure, all believing in a better tomorrow. Before they could be on their way to live the American dream, however, they first had to pass the health inspection—only required for the third class—before boarding, with the risk of being driven back if signs of any serious disease were discovered. These last Irish travelers joined Slav, Scandinavian, Chinese, or Lebanese immigrants who'd embarked in Southampton and Cherbourg. Housed in more modest cabins, they occupied the front and back of the ship, with their own dining room, smoking room, and a bar for playing cards. When they wanted to stretch their legs, members of the third-class didn't get to walk along an open deck like the wealthier passengers; instead, they walked on the aft well deck, which also served for walking the dogs.

Just like these immigrants, Juliette, Simone, and Louise were also leaving for a great adventure: for the first time, they would visit Joseph's birth country, this faraway land he so often told them about. Was it as beautiful as he said? Although a bit apprehensive, Juliette was hopeful. The first hours spent on the *Titanic* reassured her. She was no longer doubting the future as much, and was enjoying the company of her handsome husband and their adorable daughters.

> **66** Each night, the sun sank right in our eyes along the sea, making an undulating glittering pathway, a golden track charted on the surface of the ocean which our ship followed unswervingly until the sun dipped below the edge of the horizon, and the pathway ran ahead of us faster than we could steam and slipped over the edge of the skyline—as if the

sun had been a golden ball and had wound up
its thread of gold too quickly for us to follow. **"**
—Lawrence Beesley, *Titanic* survivor

"My mom was very enthusiastic," Louise recounts at the commemoration on the Cherbourg dock, on April 19, 1996. "She was describing the luxury of the ship, the quality of the music band."[24] Louise is referring to a letter written on the *Titanic* by her mother. She greatly treasures it. "Knowing what happened after, one cannot help feeling great emotion while reading this correspondence."

• • •

During the night of April 14th to 15th, 1912, in the freezing waters of the North Atlantic Ocean, off the coast of Newfoundland, unimaginable tragedy struck. Oh, the terror. The horror! "We hit an iceberg," Captain Edward John Smith announced to the radio operators. "Be ready to send a distress signal!"

While the *Titanic* sank, attempts were made at evacuation. Everywhere, the scene was horrendous. Passengers screamed. Others cried. In the melee, as the passengers tried to access a lifeboat, it was everyone for themselves, and many gave in to panic.

In the end, out of the 2,208 people on board, 1,496 perished.

"My mother, my sister and I were saved. My father was not allowed to get on a lifeboat. He did not survive." Behind her round-rimmed glasses, Louise is emotional. The ceremony on the Cherbourg dock is ending; she had not set foot on the premises since the tragedy.

She describes her father as a hero. Out of everything they told her when she was old enough to understand, this word is the only one that brings the hint of a smile on Louise's face. Her father, a hero! Her mother described the final scene to her so well that she knows each detail by heart.

• • •

The *Titanic*'s Lifeboat "Collapsible D" was towed to the *Carpathia* by Lifeboat No. 14 (not pictured).

Sinking of the *Titanic*. The lifeboats row away from the still lighted ship on April 15th 1912.

"Striking the water was like a thousand knives being driven into one's body. The temperature was twenty-eight degrees, four degrees below freezing."

—Charles Lightoller, Second Officer aboard *Titanic*

In the general panic that followed the collision between the *Titanic* and the iceberg, the Laroche family had been split. Juliette and Simone had miraculously found themselves on a lifeboat, while Joseph was still struggling on the deck with Louise, who was close to suffocating in his arms. In the indescribable scramble for survival, he protected the child by giving elbow blows and pushing back the crowd in order to make his way through. And then there was a loud exchange with a crew member, as Joseph tried to make him understand, with desperate gestures, that he had to take Louise to the lifeboat where her mother was waiting. Because there were not enough boats for everyone, the sailor would not have any of it. He was completely overwhelmed by the circumstances, but Joseph insisted. He yelled. He implored. He begged. Another sailor finally understood him in the widespread panic and grabbed Louise to bring her down.

Upon seeing his loving family reunited in the lifeboat, all ready to go, Joseph yelled a few words of relief to his wife. "See you soon, my love!... There will be space for everyone, in the boats... Take care of our little girls... See you soon!"

Those were his last recorded words.

On boat No. 8[25], Juliette, Simone, and Louise Laroche disappeared into the cold night, a few other lifeboats behind them. On boat No. 10, Antonie Mallet was holding her son André. Albert, her husband, had not been permitted to come with them.

The wait then started, between anguish and hope.

Hours later, flares lit up the sky. They were coming from the *Carpathia*[26]. The ship had changed course after receiving the distress signals from the *Titanic*.

"From all the small boats raised a rumbling. Passengers now understood that relief was near. Soon, all the survivors of the *Titanic* were aboard the *Carpathia*. Seven hundred or so. Rare were those who, among these survivors, had not left a father, a brother, a son, or a husband aboard the sinking ship," Juliette recounts. "When we asked news from the officers of the *Carpathia*, they replied: 'Don't worry! Other ships went by the *Titanic*, and are right now headed toward New York, where you will find your loved ones.' Thus, they hid the truth to the end. Not until our arrival in New York did we learn it in whole, in its horrifying reality."

. . .

In April 1996, on the Cherbourg dock where she is paying homage to the victims of the sinking, Louise knows that she's alive today because of her father, the hero. Since the tragedy, she's suffered from the absence of her savior. She can no longer remember the sound of his voice, the smell of his cologne, the feel of his hugs. She cannot remember the shape of his mustache, and she still misses him terribly.

Louise never married, and neither did Simone, both haunted by the memory of their savior, unable to overcome the loss. Louise will not often speak of it, but deep in her soul, she believes that no tenderness will ever equal that of her loving father.

Claude Carrer, the Mayor's representative, turns toward Louise and highlights in a few simple and touching words the life of this woman, one "that dramatically changed in Cherbourg." In a short speech, hiding once again behind the collective suffering of her family to avoid talking about her own pain, eighty-six-year-old Louise confides that they've all been left with terrible emotional scars. Her mother had the hardest time talking about the tragedy, and the atrocious images of that night remained with her until she died. "For example," Louise says as she stares at the headstone erected in front of her, "my mother raised us with an obsessive fear of travels."

This explains why she didn't attend the reunion organized in Boston by the *Titanic* Historical Society[27]. The Society did not take offense at Louise's absence. Incidentally, the president and founder, historian Edward Kamuda[28], is here at the Cherbourg tribute. He's heading a delegation of twelve members of the Society who, like him, traveled from the United States for the occasion.

For Carrer and for all the other people surrounding Louise, the Cherbourg tribute is important because only eight survivors of the *Titanic* remain in the world—two of them in France—to bear witness to the catastrophe. In the Laroche family, only Louise is still alive. Her sister, Simone, passed away in 1973. Their mother died in 1980.

The only other French survivor who is still alive is not present on this day. His name is Michel Navratil[29]. He was three and a half years old at the time of the tragedy, almost the same age as Simone Laroche. He was also traveling in second class with his father and his younger brother Edmond, two years old.

Michel and Edmond Navratil's father had boarded the *Titanic* under a false name. He had kidnapped his two sons from their mother, whom he was divorcing. After his death in the sinking, the two brothers became "orphans" in New York because no family came to claim them. The international media was immediately enraptured by the mystery surrounding these children. Who were they? Where were they from? Who were their parents? A daily newspaper in Quebec speculated that they were the children of... Joseph Laroche, going as far as masculinizing the names of the two biracial girls to assign them to the two white boys. On April 22, 1912, *La Patrie*[30] called the boys Louis and Simon. "New York authorities believe that Mr. and Mrs. Laroche might have been French, or maybe Canadian-French," the reporter wrote, "as they have been unable to gain information from the two boys who do not even know their last name."

Eventually, Michel and Edmond Navratil's mother, who lived in Nice, recognized her children from a picture published in the papers. On May 8, 1912, she embarked from Cherbourg to get them and bring them back home.

■ ■ ■

The Navratil boys had met the Laroche girls on the *Titanic*. But Michel and Louise had not seen each other again since the tragedy. He lived in Montpellier, and she lived in Villejuif. It was not until July 2005, six years after the Cherbourg tribute, that they met again in Paris with another survivor, the English nonagenarian Millvina Dean.[31]

RMS *Carpathia* carrying rescued *Titanic* passengers and *Titanic*'s lifeboats.

RMS *Carpathia* was a Cunard Line transatlantic passenger steamship built by Swan Hunter & Wigham Richardson in Newcastle upon Tyne, England. On her maiden voyage in 1903, *Carpathia* traveled from Liverpool to Boston. In April 1912, *Carpathia* became famous for her role in the rescue efforts following the sinking of the *Titanic*, a dangerous rescue mission that involved traveling through treacherous ice fields. *Carpathia* arrived within two hours of the *Titanic*'s sinking and rescued 705 of its survivors from lifeboats. On July 17, 1918, RMS *Carpathia* sank off the southern coast of Ireland after being torpedoed by the German submarine SM U-55.

"Icebergs loomed up and fell astern and we never slackened. It was an anxious time with the *Titanic*'s fateful experience very close in our minds. There were 700 souls on *Carpathia* and those lives as well as the survivors of the *Titanic* herself depended on the sudden turn of the wheel."

—Captain Arthur H. Rostron, Commander of *Carpathia*

"Then creeping over the edge of the sea we saw a single light and presently a second below it. It seemed almost too good to be true and I think everyone's eyes were filled with tears, men's as well as women's. All around us we heard shouts and cheers."

—Lawrence Beesley, *Titanic* Survivor

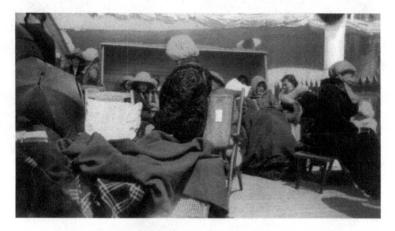

Survivors of the *Titanic* aboard the *Carpathia*, April 1912. Many were grieving widows mourning their husbands who'd gone down with the ship.

"When day broke, I saw the ice I had steamed through during the night. I shuddered, and could only think that some other hand than mine was on that helm during the night."

—Captain Arthur H. Rostron, Commander of *Carpathia*

Survivors of the sinking of the *Titanic*, Michel and Edmond Navratil, of Nice (France) sit on their mother's lap in 1912.

Michel Navratil Jr.

At three-and-a-half years old, Michel Navratil Jr. (1908-2001) was on board the *Titanic* after he and his brother Edmond were kidnapped by their father. According to *Encyclopedia Titanica*, on the night of the sinking, when their father brought Michel and Edmond to the deck, Second Officer Charles Lightoller had ordered a locked-arms circle of crew members around Collapsible D (the last and ninth lifeboat lowered on the port side) so that only women and children could get through. Navratil Sr. handed the boys through the ring of men, and reportedly gave Michel Jr. a final message: "My child, when your mother comes for you, as she surely will, tell her that I loved her dearly and still do. Tell her I expected her to follow us, so that we might all live happily together in the peace and freedom of the New World." When the boys were rescued, the international media was enraptured by the mystery surrounding them. Finally, their mother, who lived in Nice, recognized them from the papers and embarked from Cherbourg-Octeville to bring them back home. Six years after the Cherbourg tribute, the Navratil boys and Louise Laroche met again in Paris with another survivor, an English nonagenarian named Millvina Dean.

That day, Louise boarded the *Nomadic* once again. It was still in service, still in good shape. It was anchored at the foot of the Eiffel Tower. Under the glare of the cameras and photographers invited for the event, she spent a long time on the ferry that had carried her to the *Titanic* with her family. All together, the attendees toured the *Nomadic*, traveling from one deck to another, and everyone took a souvenir shot on the very well-kept lower deck. Louise and Millvina posed together on one of the benches of the *Nomadic*, and the emotion was almost palpable. Olivier Mendez, who attended the memorial, was filled with emotion as the three children of the *Titanic* shared their experience. The reporters interviewed Louise for two hours, and Millvina granted them the same time, bringing back memories and high points in her life. Michel and Louise held hands the entire time.

■ ■ ■

For a long time, Louise stayed away from tributes and commemorative events, to the point that others humorously nicknamed her "Mrs. Nyet," borrowing the Russian word for "no," because she categorically rejected any invitation to an event related to the *Titanic*. But, over the years, Louise had eventually come to accept her status as the ultimate survivor, and she finally took her role to heart, participating in this ceremony in Cherbourg and the unveiling of this headstone that commemorates Joseph Laroche, her father the hero, among the victims of the sinking.

"It is important for the memory of my family and all those who lost a loved one aboard the *Titanic*," Louise acknowledges in a soft voice, after placing bouquets of flowers at the foot of the headstone. Her face is solemn. Her features are drawn. She reminds everyone once again that her family had simply been "at the wrong place, at the wrong time." One can feel her emotion. She is lost, alone in the crowd, in a painful face-off with herself, with her life story, with the heavy burden no one has been able to relieve for all those years.

Louise will say no more. She takes a deep breath and stares one last time at the message written on the plaque that she just unveiled in honor of the 281 passengers who had boarded in Cherbourg, just like her family, the Laroches, eighty-four years ago. It reads: "RMS *Titanic*: During its maiden voyage, the liner *Titanic* made its only stopover in Cherbourg on April 10, 1912. It would go down in the night of April 14 to April 15 off the coast of Newfoundland. The *Titanic* Historical Society of Indian Orchard (Massachusetts, USA) and the city of Cherbourg commemorated this tragic event on April 19, 1996."

Louise remembers her father. She keeps a picture of him in her purse. A purse that she is holding even closer to her body, realizing again how cruel fate was to this wonderful man who loved his wife and adored his children.

Joseph Laroche was going back to his country. He never had a chance to see his homeland again.

AN IMPORTANT STORY

"The facts were there all along but were not known overseas until the Titanic Historical Society published (Olivier) Mendez's account of Louise Laroche's story in 1995, followed by (Judith) Geller's history three years later. Not long afterward, a massive Titanic exhibit at the Chicago Museum of Science and Industry sparked a June 2000 article in Ebony magazine by Zondra Hughes, titled 'What Happened to the Only Black Family on the Titanic?'"
—Henry Louis Gates Jr., 100 Amazing Facts About The Negro

"Nowhere in the copious 1912 press descriptions of the ship and the interviews with the survivors was the presence of a black family among the passengers ever mentioned."
—Judith Geller, Titanic: Women and Children First

"In the blockbuster film Titanic, Leonardo DiCaprio's role could have easily been played by a Black man—and it would have been historically accurate. In fact, the life story of Haitian native Joseph Philippe Lemercier Laroche is far more intriguing than the movie's lead character."
—Zondra Hugues, Ebony

"At times, the facts of (Joseph Laroche's) life are so powerful they feel like legend."
—Henry Louis Gates Jr., The Root

RACE, CLASS, GENDER, & THE TITANIC

"For several months Juliette Laroche and her husband Joseph had been discussing the benefits of moving from Villejuif, France, to Haiti, Joseph's country of origin. It was a great disappointment to him that having earned his engineering degree in France he could not find employment there. No matter how qualified he was, the blackness of his skin kept him from securing a position that paid his worth."

—Judith B. Geller, Titanic: Women and Children First

———————

"It is strange that nowhere in the copious 1912 press descriptions of the ship and the interviews with the survivors was the presence of a black family among the passengers ever mentioned. (...) It seems doubly strange in view of the keenness of the passengers and crew to take pot shots at other ethnic groups. This was done to such an extent that the White Star Line was forced to apologize for the derogatory statements made by Titanic's crew about the 'Italians' (a generic term for all the darker-skinned passengers) and their behavior during the last moments on the dying ship. Laroche must have escaped their vitriol and prejudice by acquitting himself at all times like the gentleman he was brought up to be"

—Judith B. Geller, Titanic: Women and Children First

———————

"While the RMS Titanic left a lasting cultural legacy, the fate of its wealthiest passengers discussed in news and entertainment media, the history of the ship's Chinese passengers has remained largely hidden. And racist policies have a lot to do with it. (...) Six Chinese guys made it off the Titanic alive and 24 hours later were written out of the story. That wasn't an accident. That was deliberate. It's something that the culture of the time made happen."

—Kimberly Yam, HuffPost

———————

"In 1912, Rep. Seaborn Roddenbery (D-GA) made a (second) attempt to revise the U.S. Constitution in order to ban interracial marriage in all fifty states. His proposed amendment read as follows: That intermarriage between negroes or persons of color and Caucasians or any other character of persons within the United States or any territory under their jurisdiction, is forever prohibited; and the term 'negro or person of color,' as here employed, shall be held to mean any and all persons of African descent or having any trace of African or negro blood.' (Of course,) later theories of physical anthropology will suggest that every human being has some African ancestry, which could have rendered this amendment unenforceable had it passed."

—Tom Head, ThoughtCo.

_____

"Racial discrimination prevented Joseph Laroche from obtaining a high-paying job in France. Since the family needed more money to cope with Louise's medical bills, Joseph decided to return to Haiti to find a better-paying engineering job, the move being planned for 1913."

—Encyclopedia Titanica

_____

"Some versions of the disaster have contended that the crew was under orders to give priority aboard lifeboats to first- and second-class passengers, and even that doors were kept locked that would have given people in steerage faster access to the lifeboats through parts of the ship dedicated to higher-paying passengers. Though these assertions have been disputed, Ms. (Millvina) Dean said that she believed them to be true, and that her father might otherwise have survived."

—John F. Burns, The New York Times

_____

"The Titanic carried enough lifeboats for only fifty-two percent of its passengers, and judging by which passengers got a seat, class clearly mattered. Some sixty-two percent of first-class passengers found places in the boats, compared with forty-one percent of second-class passengers, and twenty-five percent of steerage (or third-class) passengers. The crew fared even worse, with just twenty-four percent saved."

—Greg Daugherty, Money.com

_____

"As an interracial couple, (Joseph and Juliette Laroche probably) experienced a lot of harassment and taunts from the crew and passengers, so much so that The White Star Line, the company that owned the RSM Titanic, had to issue a public apology later for the behavior of their crew and passengers towards the Lemercier Laroche family."

—Kat St. Fort, Kreyolicious

TRUE OR FALSE

FALSE

A black woman named Malinda Borden was denied a spot in a lifeboat on the Titanic because she was black.

There's been no evidence of Malinda Borden aboard the *Titanic*.

FALSE

Some men got a spot on a lifeboat by dressing up as women.

Not only is this one not true, but it ruined the life of the men who were accused of doing it. William T. Sloper was called "Skirts" for the rest of his life, and Dickson Bishop's wife, Helen, divorced him for cross-dressing.

The 700 third-class passengers had to share two bathtubs.

TRUE

Third-class/steerage passengers were locked below to keep them from taking space in lifeboats.

FALSE

FALSE

The Titanic's strict women-and-children-first policy set an industry standard.

There had been no official order allowing only women and children to get on lifeboats. And, in a study reported by *New Scientist* of 18 modern shipwrecks and the 15,000 passengers involved, children had only about a 15 percent chance of surviving, and adult men were twice as likely to live as their female counterparts.

Mrs. Laroche and her children escaped in Lifeboat no. 8.

UNCLEAR

Boat no. 8, no. 9, or no. 14?

"Neither Madame Mallet nor Laroche could remember what number lifeboat they had escaped. The only detail Juliette remembered was that in her boat a countess or someone with a title was among those who rowed all night long. The boat had icy water in the bottom and her feet were frozen."
—Olivier Mendez, *Titanic Historical Society*

"Joseph died in the sinking but his family were saved, possibly in lifeboat 14."
—*Encyclopedia Titanica*

II. The Earth Shakes

Joseph Laroche's story began far away from Cherbourg, across the ocean—again—on a former French colony, a Caribbean island already much talked about at the time: Haiti.

He was born on May 26, 1886, in the city of Cap-Haïtien[32], in the far north of the island.

For a long time, Cap-Haïtien was the country's most important city. During colonial times and after Independence, it served as the capital of "Saint-Domingue," bustling with activities. Port-au-Prince, its great rival in the west, would later prevail, relegating Cap-Haïtien to second place. In 1886, however, with its thirteen thousand inhabitants and its active commercial port, Le Cap was still playing an important role in exchanges with Europe and North America. Ships brought flour, soap, shoes, clothes, linen, hardware, and wine. They left loaded with coffee, cocoa, wood, cotton, sugar, tortoise shells, and roots of vetiver, a plant that produces an essence sought after by perfume-makers.

Trade was the specialty of Joseph Laroche's mother, Euzélie Laroche[33], who'd built a fortune. At twenty-four, the single mother had enough money to raise her son on her own. She gave Joseph her last name because the father refused to acknowledge him.

"From what we know of her, she was a dynamic and hard-working woman. She was a speculator in sugarcane, cotton, and, above all, coffee,[34]" jurist Christina Schutt[35], a family descendant, explains with pride. "Euzélie is the sister of the great-grandfather of my ancestor," she says.

In Haiti, a speculator is a merchant who practices general business. However, if one wants to acquire agricultural commodities, one must first buy a special government license. Euzélie Laroche had this valuable permit, the key to her success; it allowed her to purchase the planters' harvest. From the coffee producers, for instance, she bought large bags.

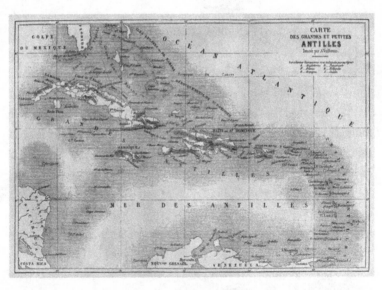

Old map of the Antilles, created by Vuillemin and Erhard, published in *Le Tour du Monde*, Paris, 1860

When rocks, dirt, and rotten fava beans slipped through, Euzélie separated the good from the bad and then reconditioned the merchandise, which she sold at her Kay-Kafé on Rue 8. The store was patronized by a specialized client base.

"There was a huge scale inside the store to weigh the bags. She sold her coffee to big local enterprises and to exporters," historian Georges Michel explains.

"She was also visited by European buyers, French and mostly German," Christina Schutt adds.

Coffee was at the time Haiti's main asset, and even its "only real currency," according to the French consul general. In 1888, two years after Joseph Laroche's birth, the country exported over seventy-five million pounds of coffee, shipped to Le Havre. Trading with Le Havre, New York, or Hamburg allowed the local economy to remain sustainable and benefited numerous families. While the big planters could easily grow rich from the business, it was not always the case for the small farmers, however. Most of the time, they had to go through multiple middlemen to move their product. They sold the coffee through a trading network of Haitian businesswomen, also called "acrobats," "submarines," or "*Madan sara*."[36] The latter resold the coffee to speculators, who finally brought it to their customers.

According to an official report, "the distribution network was far from linear, because the producers also had direct contact with speculators when they sold them their ground coffee." Euzélie Laroche preferred procuring directly from the source. This way, she said, everybody wins.

This complex system, put in place by a government that also collected taxes, lasted until 1996. That year, there were two hundred thousand planters, ten thousand acrobats, submarines and *madan-sarah*, seven hundred speculators, and seven exporters in Haiti. That's why a minister said: "Coffee is a gold mine for everyone, except its producers."

■ ■

Euzélie Laroche was born 160 kilometers from Le Cap, in the municipality of Grande Rivière du Nord[37]. She later moved to Le Cap with her mother, who was in search of employment, and Euzélie rapidly adapted to the rhythm of this port city. In fact, Euzélie took the plunge almost immediately, creating her own business, as she wanted independence; she refused to be like the single mothers around her whose sole occupation in life was to raise their children, alone.

In the streets of Grande Rivière du Nord, Euzélie had more than once observed merchant women selling the cheap junk they procured from some local wholesaler. She felt she had it in her to do the same—only better. Buy and sell: it was even easier in a port city like Le Cap, where trade was a tradition.

Founded in 1670 by buccaneers, Cap Français, as it was called in old times, was the heart and soul of the sugar industry. Under the whip, enslaved men and women planted and harvested sugarcane, which the masters sold for their exclusive benefit.

In January 1802, however, the tide had turned. The slaves had eventually rebelled and chased the colonizers away. Then, everything had changed. Well, almost everything.

"The violent separation of the colony from the home country was immediately followed by an embargo that put a stop to all exchange between France and Haiti," historian Benoît Joachim says. "This greatly benefited the British, who refused to side with the Napoleonic empire and its economic strangulation of the new state."

The British were not the only ones to take advantage of the new regime. The Germans also continued business with this small, now independent, country. Many of their nationals had been established as traders or merchants since the eighteenth century. In 1841, one of their own, Peter Gottlieb[38], disembarked in Le Cap. He was nineteen years old and dreaming of adventure.

Cap Français

Founded in 1670 by buccaneers, Cap Français, as it was called in old times, was the heart and soul of the sugar industry. Under the whip, enslaved men and women planted and harvested sugarcane, which the masters sold for their exclusive benefit. In this picture: The massacre of French colonists and burning of Cap Français in 1820

"The German sailor, Peter Gottlieb, was often seen in the Hamburg port, coming back with vivid stories of lands where anything could be undertaken. The Germans who settled in Haiti were welcome, and it seemed to him the ideal place to start a new life," Christina Schutt explains about her ancestor.

Peter Gottlieb left gripping testimony of the earthquake[39] that devasted Le Cap a year after his arrival, on May 7, 1842. The city had twenty-seven east-west streets crossing at right angles; nineteen north-south streets. The houses had two or three stories. The first floor usually served as a shop or stable. The upper floors were residences.

"I felt terrible anxiety and pain during the ten hours I was stuck under the rubble and beams. My left arm was completely buried, and my body was stuck under the stairs. A big rock on my chest threatened to stop my breathing," Peter Gottlieb recounted. Nevertheless, he was able to free himself after tremendous effort.

"I finally got around four o'clock in the morning to the beach, where there was a crowd of people, some praying and others crying or screaming of pain from their serious injuries. The city was in total ruin and what had not burnt had been plundered. Indeed, the very first day, bandits appeared from the inner country. They stole everything they could find since military order had disappeared."

Half of the nine thousand inhabitants of Le Cap perished in the catastrophe. Henri Laroche[40], father of Euzélie and grandfather of Joseph, lost two children. Survivors fled to neighboring localities. But a year later, braving their fear, many of them came back. Little by little, Le Cap was rebuilt. Trade resumed gradually. The economy restarted.

▪ ▪ ▪

Morning at the Cathédrale Notre-Dame de l'Assomption in Cap-Haïtien, Haiti.

Cap-Haïtien is a port city in the mountainous north coast region of Haiti. It was founded in 1670 by the French and was originally known as Cap-Français. It gained early renown as the "Paris of the Antilles" for its stunning architecture and cultural offerings. It served as capital of Saint-Domingue until 1770 and was the scene of slave uprisings in 1791. The city was razed by French and Haitian troops in 1802 but was later rebuilt under the reign of King Henri Christophe. After the revolution (around 1820), he proclaimed it the capital of the Northern Kingdom of Haiti. Cap-Haïtien was Haiti's most important city for a long time until Port-au-Prince relegated it to second place. Joseph Laroche was born in Cap-Haïtien, which is often referred as Le Cap or Okap.

Cockfights.

On some afternoons, Joseph attended cockfights in an open-air arena in the outskirts of the city. The gamblers crammed around a circle to watch two gallinaceans furiously trash each other by striking though the feathers with reinforced spurs.

Cockfighting is an ancient spectator sport that can be traced back at least 6,000 years. It was popular in Persia, India, and China, and spread northward into Europe after being introduced to Greece between 524-460, BC. Eventually, colonization and the transatlantic slave trade introduced it to the Western hemisphere. Cockfighting plays a central role in Alex Haley's novel *Roots*. In cockfights, specially bred gamecocks are equipped with metal spurs or knives, which are fastened over their natural leg spurs, and are released into a circular ring where they spar off against other gamecocks, often until one of the birds dies from their injuries. Cockfighting is illegal in most of the modern world but is still a popular pastime for many spectators who place bets on the outcome of the fighting matches. As a youngster in Haiti, Joseph often attended cockfights in open air arenas.

While managing her business, Euzélie Laroche did not neglect her son. They had a special bond. First, because he was her only child, and moreover, because he was a boy—her greatest wish—with an origin story similar to her own. When she was born, her father had not acknowledged his paternity, either. However, he'd changed his mind three years later and filed a declaration of paternity in the civil registry. Euzélie knew that Joseph's father would eventually relent and legally recognize him, one day or another. In the meantime, she made sure her son got the best education possible. She wanted to make him an independent man who would not depend on anyone's goodwill. She wanted to give him the best chances to succeed in a country where poverty prevailed.

In the beautiful house where they lived in Le Cap, a maid looked after Joseph when Euzélie was absent. When there was no school, it was out of the question to let him hang around outside. Bad habits, the mother feared, are too easily adopted. Of course, it was also out of the question to isolate him from his friends in the neighborhood, all the more because they were from good families. A child must also have fun. Homework did not prevent time for soccer, jacks, or marble games.

The Laroche boy was not, by nature, very talkative. But at the mere mention of marbles, he perked up. He liked to challenge his friends in a good game and make a clean sweep of his opponent's treasure. Doomed was the one who lost; he'd go home with his head down and swear to take revenge as soon as possible. However, to save face, the loser could redeem himself in a race. The small group rushed forward. Whoever first reached the Hyppolite Bridge that crossed the river was declared the winner. This was not Joseph's favorite exercise. He was not a gifted sprinter, despite what his pals might have thought. They begged him to let them have a lead; they believed him to have the upper hand because the bridge was built by...a Laroche!

Joseph's childhood was a time of innocence and freedom from care, a time for discovery and initiation into traditions. Surrounded by his mother and by youngsters his age, Joseph lived an existence that brimmed with the energy, the vitality, the essence of his country.

On some afternoons, he attended cockfights[41] in an open-air arena in the outskirts of the city. The gamblers crammed around a circle to watch two gallinaceans furiously trash each other by striking though the feathers with reinforced spurs. "I like when the rooster gets mean," an old man explained to Joseph, the first time he came. "When two mean roosters face off, that makes for an entertaining fight. It is very interesting to see them switch from defense to attack mode." He added, "You know, my boy, this is a metaphor for our own Haitian identity."

Sometimes too, after dark, the Laroche boy attended story-telling evenings, mostly held on Saturdays. Historian Claude Dauphin explains that "stories play a fundamental role in building the Haitian child's imaginary world. It is inseparable from Voodoo, theater, and music, and sometimes musicians accompany the teller. These stories come alive, thanks to the master storyteller's virtuosity, and transport the audience to a fantastic, magical world."

Men, women, and children gathered in a crowded courtyard, standing or seated on the ground. The stories captivated the audience, suspended between past and present. Everyone laughed, exchanged pleasantries, and let go of all worries. "*Krik!*"[42] the storyteller started fervently. "*Krak!*" the crowd replied right away.

Then began a beautiful journey into the past through stories of Bouki and Malice.[43] Through their adventures, crafty animals like Anansi[44] and Brother Rabbit[45] taught Joseph that, in life, the shrewder ones often win.

But more than the stories and the roosters and the games with other boys, what Joseph Laroche loved above all else were those moments he spent with his mother. Whenever she stepped away from her business, he could enjoy her company. He liked having her all to himself. She congratulated him on his good grades as he excitedly told her about school. On the playground, he explained, other children made fun of him—all on account of his grandfather, believed to have practically populated the whole of Le

Cap by himself. Euzélie Laroche burst into laughter, just like every time someone reminded her how extraordinarily fertile her father had been. Yes, it was true: Henri Laroche was a ladies' man. He was charming and attractive and was not afraid to try his hand at marriage—over and over. The result? Upon his death, in 1876, he left behind "between twenty-eight and thirty children," among them Euzélie, and about sixty grandchildren, among them Joseph. It's become impossible to count the number of Laroche descendants in Le Cap. But as Christina Schutt points out, Henri Laroche never walked away from his responsibilities. "He eventually acknowledged all of his children, something many men did not do at the time in Le Cap, or anywhere else in Haiti. He'd go to City Hall and legally recognize the children in small groups of five. It was quite peculiar."

● ● ●

Euzélie wished her father were still alive to pass his valuable knowledge to his grandson, as tradition required. He would have told him the history of his family and his country. With Henri Laroche gone, Joseph's grandmother Louisette took on the job of sharing the family lore every time she stopped by the house.

Louisette—whom everybody affectionately nicknamed Lisettine—was a down-to-earth and honest woman who worked as an ironer, an occupation that required strong arms and legs. She walked several miles every day to pick up bundles of clean linen from the rich families in Le Cap. She smoothed out and carefully folded the linen at home, before making the return trip to the owners' houses for delivery and compensation. Although she did not get paid much, "all work is noble," Lisettine told Joseph, showing him an iron box filled with hot coal. Thanks to her work tool, this old box purchased long ago with her meager savings, she had raised with dignity the two children she had with Henri Laroche before their separation: Euzélie, born in 1862, and Bertrand, born in 1865.

For Joseph, Lisettine's visits were always enchanting, even though she never failed to grumble a little while passing the threshold. She found fault with the house, which she deemed unclean, or with the food, which she believed left a lot to be desired. She reprimanded the maid for a fork stored with the spoons, or a bedsheet placed on the wrong shelf. She inspected every room, every piece of furniture, and noticed the thinnest layer of dust. Nothing ever met her approval.

Although Joseph feared his grandmother's strict rules, remnants from the hard life she'd lived in the past, he nevertheless loved her very much—for her kindness and for the stories she shared about his family and Le Cap. Some of these stories, he'd heard a thousand times, and yet he did not tire of them. He asked to hear them again.

"Your great-grandfather, Henry Laroche, was a white man," Lisettine began in a high-pitch voice, "a soldier in a garrison here in the north." She continued, "One day he came across a free woman of color. She turned his head." Lisettine asked, "Do you know what a free woman of color is?" (Joseph shook his head, eager to hear what happened next.) "Well, it means that this black woman was no longer a slave, as opposed to the rest of the black population. Her name was Hellène François. She liked Henry Laroche, and he liked her back." Lisettine smiled. "So, they knew each other in the biblical sense and that is how your grandfather was born." She became pensive. "But during that time, even when they were not slaves, people worked with their hands as much as with their head. And because your grandfather did both well, he rapidly learned the craft of shoemaker. You see these leather shoes you are wearing? Well, he made things like that."

As her mother revived the memory of the late Henry Laroche, Euzélie watched her son's eyes light up. Both Euzélie and Lisettine answered Joseph's questions with candor. The boy was curious about everything, and his mother appreciated that. Was it not the sign of a brilliant mind? He would go far. That was a certain. His mother believed it.

■ ■ ■

Only once did Euzélie elude Joseph's questions. That night, as it was getting late, Joseph was worried about his mother, who still hadn't returned home. He paced the house, irritable and impatient. When she eventually returned, she didn't return his hug. She remained silent. When he tried a smile, she kept her stony expression. He understood that something serious, even terrible, had happened. But what? He remained in the dark until the next day, when, during mass, the priest in his homily asked the believers "to pray for the victims of the sinking."

Joseph didn't know what the word _sinking_ meant, but he could read consternation on everybody's faces. What did it mean? Why was it so painful? The boy would not wonder for very long. From his pulpit, the vicar enlightened him by describing the dreadful scene of a liner sinking in the ocean.

The liner in question was the _Ville de Saint-Nazaire_[46] in route from New York. Laded with merchandise for the West Indies, it was to stop over in Le Cap on March 6, 1897. It never arrived. It went down due to a leak, worsened by a violent storm. Among the eleven passengers and seventy-four crewmen aboard, only eighteen people survived. As Joseph listened to the macabre account of the sinking, he pondered the stories he'd been told about the animal world, where only the shrewder one played his cards right. Was it the same for humans? Were the survivors luckier, or simply more astute, than those who'd drowned?

■ ■ ■

Answers to Joseph's questions came from a Martinican survivor, sailor Marcel Héber-Suffrin.[47] He explained that, the entire night, the crew used big buckets to try to empty the engine room. But at seven in the morning, "all hope to save the ship was lost." When the captain ordered the evacuation of the _Ville de Saint-Nazaire,_ boarding the three lifeboats and the dinghy was extremely difficult. "They had to strap down the women," Marcel Héber-Suffrin said, "because the wild sea terrified them. Using a hoist, they hauled down the human cargo into the small boats. After a ninety-minute operation, they had been able to squeeze twenty-one people in the first lifeboat that then set off to the high seas."

The men were rowing. The storm was not waning. The sea was "furious." It was cold. After four days, fatigue, hunger, and thirst "started to have a disastrous impact on morale." Unable to stand it any longer, a boy "profusely" drank salted water.[48] Soon, he was rambling and wanted to throw himself in the ocean. "After a few hours of agony, he breathed his last breath."

A man also died that evening, and then a woman the following night. "From the moment she got on the boat," Héber-Suffrin said, "she sat on the edge. We provided her with all the care we could, but the violent waves kept her constantly drenched and helpless. It was torturous for her.

Her moans, moments before she died, broke our hearts. She extended her arms toward us, mouth open, her voice raspy. The water ultimately choked down her whimpers, and she died in agony."

The next day, a man jumped into the ocean. The captain sobbed, disheartened, calling over and over for his wife and five little girls, whom he would never see again.

Héber-Suffrin was rescued *in extremis* by a passing ship. He later found out about the ordeal of the people evacuated in the two other lifeboats.

In one boat, the madness started on the third day in open sea. From that point on, not one day went by without four or five "poor souls" going insane and jumping into the ocean. In the other one, many were driven to incredible acts of lechery that should forever remain untold. As for the dinghy, it disappeared with everyone on board.

■ ■ ■

The sinking of the *Ville de Saint-Nazaire* created heartbreak in Le Cap because the locals loved to welcome the ships that regularly stopped over at the port. They came from America, France, Germany, and even Denmark, carrying all kinds of products that brought happiness to the young and the old alike.

The liner *Franconia*[49] was one of the star ships of the time. Starting in 1874, it regularly set sail from Hamburg, headed to the West Indies, until the new owners changed its name to *Olindes Rodrigues*. For a while, the ship traveled between different local ports in France, until 1891, when it was assigned a new itinerary: Le Havre-Haiti. Historian Marc Péan explains that, "every month, whenever the liner *Olindes Rodrigues* arrived in Le Cap, the local joined in celebration. A converted cabin on board the ship held a very large selection of magazines and books, from the last Zola,[50] Loti,[51] or Bourget[52] novels, to other political, economic, and scientific works." These books and magazines brought happiness to the teachers, lawyers, or reporters who were members of various literary clubs in Le Cap. They regularly met to talk about literature, music, or philosophy, in the home of wealthy merchant Larante Desormeaux or famous physician Nemours Auguste, an uncle of Joseph Laroche.

The ships that stopped in Le Cap were usually freight vessels that had been remodeled to hold a few passengers. The journey was long and grueling. In bad sailing conditions, the crossing between Le Cap and New York could take up to seventy days. Christina Schutt relates that, "during the many storms that sometimes lasted for days, passengers were confined to their quarters, crammed in filth and stink, with no light—to avoid the risk of fire—and no access to the deck. Windows remained tightly closed to protect against large waves. Some ships, however, had cabins for the passengers of more fortunate means." And it is in one of those cabins, on board one of those ships, that Joseph Laroche would soon leave Haiti to continue his studies in France. His mother gave in to the trend: wealthy Le Cap families often spent a fortune to send their children to Paris, as there was no university in Haiti at the time.

Émile Zola.

Literary master Émile Zola (1840–1902), who spearheaded the development of theatrical naturalism, failed his *baccalauréat* examination not once, but twice! That goes to show you: Even if you may not be a good student, you can still be successful in literature...or in life. Many famous authors of the nineteenth century lived on almost nothing, as their works were not recognized when they were alive. Zola actually made quite a bite of money as a writer during his lifetime.

...

For Joseph, the countdown started a month after the *Ville de Saint-Nazaire* tragedy.

At dinner one evening, his mother announced that she had saved enough money for his passage to France, where he would attend school. His future was set. It was just a matter of time, Joseph knew, and the excitement kept him awake that night.

And for good reason: Many of his friends dreamed of traveling across the ocean to visit—and even live in—France. It had been his own secret wish, even though he never talked about it. From a distance, he'd succumbed to the charms of that faraway land, as the adults often praised its beauty and its culture. The France they talked about seemed different in its sophistication from the cruel one their ancestors had fought against during the independence wars, and whenever Joseph met a "Parisian" in Le Cap, such as his uncle, Nemours Auguste, he understood how one could be fulfilled by a stay in France. In fact, Nemours Auguste was one of the most noteworthy figures of the time. Historian Marc Péan reports that, in many respects, Auguste held a groundbreaking position. A physician who'd graduated from the Medical School of Paris, he was a very good practitioner who was praised everywhere for his know-how and his remarkable cures.

For a long while, Joseph dreamed good dreams of Europe. However, he acquired mixed emotions when reality set in and his departure date was set. He felt both joy and sadness at the idea of leaving his family, his friends, and his city. Was it worth it? Could he not succeed in life if he stayed in his country? For the first time in his young life, he questioned his mother's choice for him. But since her decision was made, Joseph wondered if other parents would consider a group departure. It would be so much better if other children his age were to embark on the journey with him. Once in France, they could then help and encourage each other.

The idea was appealing, but there was one problem: 241 Le Cap children were born like Joseph in 1886. How many of these parents could afford such a trip? Most students ended their education after secondary school, including Luc Grimard. The orphan did not allow his life circumstances to stop him from succeeding, however. He later established himself as one of the greatest writers of his generation.

• • •

Since the sinking of the *Ville de Saint-Nazaire*, Joseph Laroche was rattled. Despite himself, he had become obsessed with the destiny of broken ships, as if a small lamp was lit in his head to shine light on the submerged wrecks and pull them from oblivion by bringing them back to the surface. He had no doubt that, even before the *Ville de Saint-Nazaire,* he had gotten wind of at least one other maritime catastrophe; probably due to a lack of understanding, he had not really paid attention to then. Today, everything was different. Today, he was well aware of what could happen to one at sea. He couldn't think of anything else. Or picture anything else. Or hear anything else. Even in Joseph's history class, the topic of the sinking disaster haunted him. The teacher conducted a lesson about Christopher Columbus, a white seafarer who had arrived in Haiti in December 1492, before colonization, with three large caravels. When one of these ships, the *Santa Maria,*[53] sank off the coast of Le Cap, the first-contacted Native Americans aided the crewmen; together, they built a fort with the ship's debris. When he left the island, Christopher Columbus left behind forty-something comrades. The latter committed so many abuses that their fed-up hosts slaughtered them.

Christopher Columbus (1451-1506).

The Landing of Columbus. Painting by Currier & Ives, 1846.

Santa Maria.

Christopher Columbus's caravels. The *Santa Maria* sank off the coast of Le Cap. According to Jonny Wikes, a contributor to the website *History Revealed*, "it is widely believed that the crews of the *Santa Maria, Nina,* and *Pinta* were mostly made up of criminals. Although it is true that a royal decree in Spain offered amnesty to any criminals who joined the voyage, only four men were actually convicts."

VOLUME XCIIL—NO. 29.   THE RECORD-UNION   PAGE 2

WRECK OF THE STEAMER

VILLE DE ST. NAZAIRE.

A BOAT BELONGING TO THE ill-FATED VESSEL PICKED UP AT SEA.

In It Were Found Six Dead Bodies in a Heap Under the Seats.

All of Which Were Washed Overboard and Sank When the Boat Was Being Hoisted on Board the Steamer Creole.

Also Reported That Another Steamship Rescued Sixteen Survivors of the Wrecked Vessel.

NEW YORK, March 22.—The Cromwell line steamer Creole, Captain Gager, from New Orleans, which arrived today, reports that on the passage a boat belonging to the ill-fate-d steamer Ville de St. Nazaire, which foundered off Hatteras on Monday, March 8th, was picked up with six dead bodies in it.

Captain Gager said that in latitude 36.7, longitude 47.10, a boat was passed filled with water. After going a short distance he recalled the loss of the St. Nazaire, and thinking it might belong to her, turned the steamer and put back. When the steamer got alongside the boat it was seen that she contained six bodies lying in a heap under the seats, and the water in her was up to the gunwhale. The davits were not strong enough to hoist her out of the water, so the forward derrick was swung over the side and the boatswain was sent down to hook on the tackle.

The tackle was first hooked to the bow, and, hoisting the boat so as to empty some of the water out of her, the bodies were washed out of the other end and sank immediately.

The boat was taken on board the Creole and brought to port, and now lies on the steamer's dock awaiting the orders of the French steamship company. The boat contained some clothing, mostly seamen's trousers and jumpers, two women's shoes of different patterns, a child's sock, a nipple to a nursing bottle, part of a bottle of soothing syrup, and some claret bottles containing fresh water. There was also quite a quantity of French bread, two caseknives and a uniform button of the French company's service.

There is some doubt as to one of the bodies being that of a woman. The man who went down into the boat says there was no woman, while some of the excited passengers who crowded about looking at the ghastly spectacle said there was, and the mate was ready to swear he saw a woman's body. Captain Gager says there was not a woman, and he thinks from the dress and appearance of the bodies that they were part of the crew, and that two of them were colored men. The boat is a large one, about forty feet long, and pointed at both ends. She had the appearance of being quite old, and is very much dilapidated, probably caused by the buffeting of the waves during the thirteen days she had been in the water since the wreck. She had no oars, mast or sail when picked up.

The survivors of the wrecked St. Nazaire who were brought to this port are having a hard struggle to regain their health, Captain Berri, Surgeon Maire and Engineer Sauts are still confined to their looms in the Hotel Martin. Their condition is somewhat improved. Slow progress is also reported in the condition of the surviving passenger, Juan de Tejada.

Recreation of an article from the *Sacramento Daily Union*, Volume 93, Number 29, 23 March 1897

A few months later, again in history class, Joseph heard about other sinking ships. He learned that, during the slave trade, at least ten ships disappeared off the shores of Le Cap or in Haitian waters, causing the death of hundreds of slaves chained at the bottom of the hold. The last known sinking had happened on August 27, 1775, when the *Saint-Guillaume*[54] was coming back from Guinea with 660 slaves on board. Following a navigational error, the ship hit a reef. It was submerged by raging waters, Joseph was told, and the young man began to feel dread about his upcoming trip. These historic facts horrified him. How could he get peacefully onto a boat, knowing that it might go underwater? Land offered safety. Was it really reasonable to go to sea and put oneself in danger? Shaking off the fear, Joseph reassured himself with the thought that, after all, with the great advancements of technology, sailing was now safer. Even God could not sink today's liners. Anyway, why would He do such a thing? The Laroches were good Christians, from grandfather to grandson.

. . .

Five months after the sinking of the *Ville de Saint-Nazaire*, Euzélie Laroche was smiling again: Joseph's doubts had subsided. He told himself that there was no point in being scared so soon of a trip that would not happen for years. He was only eleven years old; college was not around the corner. He might as well have fun. "What must happen will happen," he thought. "It's up to fate."

But often, it is during those times of boyish insouciance, when life quietly goes on, that the unexpected suddenly happens. The bad news comes: Tragedy has struck. And what tragedy in this case! On August 4, 1897, a little after eleven thirty in the morning, the news spread like wildfire. It traveled from house to house, from neighborhood to neighborhood, across the city: Bertrand Laroche[55] was dead. He'd just ended his own life. When she learned of her brother's suicide, Euzélie was crushed. She had not seen it coming. Pain and consternation gripped her heart. She didn't understand.

How can one die at thirty-two years old? Of course, her brother's business as a speculator came with some difficulties—the falling price of the coffee was affecting everyone, including Euzélie—but... suicide? She wondered what had really driven him to such an irreparable act. Maybe a woman had broken his heart? "That's still no reason to kill oneself," Joseph's mother said with sadness, recalling another suicide that had shaken the family seven years earlier. Her nephew, poet Arnold Laroche,[56] had killed himself in Paris. When Euzélie had learned about Arnold, he'd already been buried in the family vault at the Père-Lachaise cemetery for several months, which had added to her distress.

During those years, mail services were by ship and as slow as one can imagine. There were no telephones in Le Cap. The telephone company only became operational in 1893, shortly after the installation of the first street lights.

Joseph was shocked by the sudden death of Uncle Bertrand, who had taught him how to swim and spoiled him every time he visited. He was stunned and saddened. He couldn't believe it. "Why?" he wondered. "Why would he do that?" No one knew. Not even his grandmother, who often told him about colonial times, when the enslaved Africans sometimes chose to hang themselves rather than continue serving a master. Suicide was a way for those men to free themselves, a passage back to Africa: they believed that death would take them back to the motherland, where they would be reunited with the parents from whom they had been torn. Because of the feverish desperation in which they lived, it made sense for enslaved men to contemplate suicide, Joseph thought, although at his age these concepts were still a little over his head. In the case of Uncle Bertrand, though, he couldn't understand the willful, self-inflicted death of a man who'd been deeply loved, and whose family lived right here, in this country, in Haiti.

The wake for Bertrand Laroche became the occasion for a big family reunion, as such circumstances usually warranted. The entire family gathered in the house where he'd lived, at the corner of Rue Royale and Rue du Hasard.

The women, assembled around the body, prayed the rosary and sang hymns.

One after the other, Joseph's uncles, aunts, and cousins approached the coffin to sprinkle it with a few drops of holy water. Earlier in the afternoon, Euzélie had somehow managed to acquire the vial of precious liquid. Joseph wondered how she obtained it, considering that Bertrand, for having committed suicide, was not allowed a religious funeral service, but Euzélie wouldn't speak of the details. "I just want him to have a good journey back to his Maker," she whispered in her son's ear. "Your uncle was a wonderful person. We will miss him a lot, but I believe he will be happier where he is going," she added, while the last "Hail Mary" faded away to make way for the celebration.

In small groups here and there, they could all finally relax. As required by tradition, everyone told jokes and shared stories, recounting the deceased's life; they played dominoes and sang, ate and drank, and had fun. Euzélie went from one group to another. She talked quietly, smiled and brought comfort. Despite the circumstances, she was glad to see Amétisse Albaret, wife of Dr. Nemours Auguste,[57] the half-brother of Joseph's father. She still considered Nemours to be her "brother-in-law" and she liked Amétisse, who was none other than the daughter of Euzélie's own half-sister, Edelmonde Laroche. Consanguineous marriages were common in Le Cap at the time. "There was a lot of cross-breeding," Christina Schutt explains. "I spent several years gathering information about various families, trying to understand the links between them."

Euzélie was also delighted to see her nephew, soldier François Beaufossé Laroche, whom she loved very much and was very close to. They had no secrets from each other. She was the only one who knew of the great ambitions he had for himself and his country. Indeed, François Beaufossé Laroche[58] would climb the military and civilian ladders to the top, first becoming a general and then minister of defense. In 1913, he would try his luck at the presidential election. But the parliament members, called to decide between four competing candidates, would only give him five votes. Michel Oreste[59] would get the other seventy-two votes and, therefore, win the election.

Standing apart, Joseph was observing his mother out of the corner of his eye. Was it her cousin's budding career that put Euzélie in such good mood at the wake? Was it the glass of liquor she'd allowed herself? Was she plunged in a daze because she feared the next day, the burial, the final separation from her brother? Whatever it was, Euzélie was radiant. Her formal businesswoman persona had been replaced by that of a friendly woman—pleasant, adorable, even. Since the end of her affair with Raoul Auguste,[60] Euzélie had erected a barrier between herself and men. But here, at the wake, the barrier was down. She was beautiful, attractive, and vulnerable, and loved by everyone, Joseph realized. He was jealous. He wondered: When he did travel to Europe, would he still keep her affection? Wouldn't she forget about him and pledge all of her tenderness to a man or to the neighborhood children, who affectionately called her "Zélie?" For the first time, Joseph questioned his relationship with his mother. But, very quickly, he swept away his doubts with a shake of the head. He suddenly felt guilty for being selfish and ignoring the fact that she would suffer from his absence as well, and thought it probably best to re-immerse himself in the ambience of the wake. He loved the feeling of community and the atmosphere of celebration. He rarely saw many of these people, and yet knew he was profoundly attached to them. They were his family—a beautiful family, dispersed in all corners of the city that Joseph would soon leave.

The following afternoon, everyone dressed in black and white to bury Bertrand Laroche in the small cemetery in Le Cap. A song arose from the crowd, sad and repetitive. As Joseph listened to the melody for the first time, his thoughts were scattered. The young man was grieving. He was crying. The coffin was already covered with a shovelful of soil while the choir sang louder:

My God closer to You, closer to You...
It is the cry of my faith...
Closer to You.

Bertrand Laroche

On August 4, 1897, a little after eleven thirty in the morning, the news spread like wildfire. It traveled from house to house, from neighborhood to neighborhood, across the city: Bertrand Laroche was dead.

III. King Christophe

When Joseph Laroche bade farewell to his uncle in August 1897, Haiti had been independent for less than a century. The Haitians had won their freedom fair and square, after a series of long battles, weapons in hand. To maintain peace with France, however, the new nation was to pay ninety million gold francs to "indemnify" the former colonists. Forced to settle this amount, Haiti borrowed from big Parisian banks that would bleed it dry for 125 years. In 1895, although the young state had not yet cleared its balance, it contracted another loan of fifty million francs to relieve itself from another debt. But this time, unbeknownst to the people, part of this new loan landed in the pockets of some shady politicians.

Corruption is endemic in Haiti. Since its accession to sovereignty, the country's financial resources have been regularly plundered. The country is caught in a vicious circle, and the multitude of people living in poverty pay the price of bad faith and mismanagement. For them, one thing remains clear: the hard-earned independence—that they still would not renounce for anything in the world—has yet to serve their interests. The chains might have disappeared, but the new order is perpetuating the same iniquities as the old. Months, years, and centuries may have passed, but the inequalities remain. The blacks and the mulattos (people with both black and white ancestry) have replaced the colonists and adopted their predatory ways.

The first victims of the widespread poverty are the children. In the rare instance that these children do go to school, they wake up at dawn and walk several miles. The meager maize porridge they've had for breakfast is often the day's only sustenance. In the evening, back in the village, they prepare dinner, clean the house, do the laundry, pick up wood, sometimes also take care of goats, until, exhausted, they finally get to do some homework by the light of a kerosene lamp.

Letters left by Joseph Laroche show that, not only did he understand the complexity of Haitian realities, his astute

observations allowed him to appreciate his good fortune: he'd been born in a family that wanted for nothing.

His mother made a good living. And so did his father, Raoul Auguste, although Joseph rarely saw him. Just like Euzélie, Auguste was a "food speculator." He bought coffee, cocoa, and bitter orange peel from the farmers and sold the products in European markets. One of his most important customers was a French liqueur manufacturer, the famous Grand Marnier.

Louis Price-Mars,[61] the first Haitian psychiatrist, explains:

"Raoul Auguste was one of our most important importers and exporters. He remained for a while the king of trade at the southern entrance of Le Cap, in the part of the city that was most populated and most active for local businesses."

For Joseph Laroche, whatever people said about Raoul Auguste, good or bad, it didn't change the fact that their relationship remained at a standstill: from the moment Joseph was born, his father had refused to acknowledge his paternity, as opposed to the three other children he later had with his spouse Nesida Montreuil. In a small city like Le Cap, where everyone unavoidably ran into each other, it was hard to be ignored by someone who shared the same blood. It broke Joseph's heart. He easily pictured himself playing the role of big brother for Nina and Marguerite Auguste, born one and two years after him, not to mention the secrets he would have liked to share with little Paul Auguste.

This situation pained Euzélie enormously, for, having experienced it, she knew how it felt to be rejected by one's father. To give one's last name to a child is to give him or her the courage to face tomorrow's hardship. Euzélie wished Raoul understood all this and would, at last, get closer to his son, who would soon turn fourteen years old. She knew that, although Joseph rarely spoke of it, he was bitter. Indeed, Joseph was at a loss: How could a father inflict on his son the very ordeal he was spared? Raoul's situation mirrored Joseph's on many aspects: Raoul was his mother's only son, and Raoul's father was a married man.

Raoul Auguste

Just like Euzélie, Raoul Auguste was a "food speculator." He bought coffee, cocoa, and bitter orange peel from the farmers and sold the products in European markets. One of his most important customers was a French liqueur manufacturer, the famous Grand Marnier.

The big difference, however, was that Raoul's father had legally declared him. He'd also given his last name to Raoul, just like he had to his eleven legitimate children.

In fact, among these eleven legitimate children was his father's half-brother, Dr. Nemours Auguste, who had married Amétisse Albaret, daughter of Edelmonde Laroche, Euzélie's half-sister. This complicated things and interfered even more with Joseph's relationship with the paternal clan, as he socialized with some members and not with others.

Nemours Auguste was an elegant and erudite physician who was also an astute businessman. Backed by French investors, Nemours had proposed a railway project that was well received from the get-go by the government. The 250-kilometer network would go from Le Cap to a dozen municipalities in the area: Ouannaminthe, Trou, Vallière, La Grande Rivière, Saint-Michel de l'Attalaye, Saint-Raphaël, Hinche, Limbé, Port-Marigot, Plaisance, Marmelade, and Gonaïves. The project was certainly ambitious, budgeted at 175,000 francs per kilometer. The government worried that it might be too expensive, particularly when the finance minister, Anténor Firmin,[62] who was also from Le Cap, pointed out that France had only disbursed 40,000 francs per kilometer for its own network. In the end, the contract was broken. Pulled from Nemours, the project, however, was not abandoned. In January 1899, an incorporated company was created to take it over. Joseph's uncle was disappointed but not discontented for having shaken things up, as he feared that Le Cap was being left further behind by its competitor, Port-au-Prince, whose transportation system perfectly illustrated the gap between the two cities.

Just like the great capitals of the world, Port-au-Prince had its own tramway. In 1878, the first line was built by an American company that subsequently went bankrupt. An international consortium combining Haitian, Belgian, French, German and American capital then took over. The consortium renovated the old network and inaugurated a second line. Within six months, these networks transported about 250,000 passengers. Drawing on its success, the consortium had just opened two railway lines toward the cities of Léogâne and Manneville, respectively thirty-six and forty-three kilometers from Port-au-Prince. And if Port-au-Prince was capable of executing such projects, why not Le Cap? Why not build a railroad that linked the two big cities? It would be of great advantage for the country's trade and development. It was a daring challenge but, like Nemours Auguste, Joseph Laroche thought that it was possible.

. . .

In Joseph Laroche's family there were also renowned politicians, such as the husband of his beloved cousin Joséphine Laroche. Cincinnatus Leconte[63] was the grandson of Jean-Jacques Dessalines, the "Father of Independence." After completing his studies in Germany, he became head of the customs office in Le Cap, and later successfully built a bakery and a brickyard. In 1881, at only twenty-seven years of age, Cincinnatus Leconte was elected deputy. In 1897, he entered the government as State Secretary of Public Works. In 1911, he was elected President of the Republic: a compelling ascent for this man known for "his cold boldness and great prudence."

When Joseph Laroche visited Joséphine in 1897, as he often did in the beautiful villa where she lived with her husband at the entrance of Le Cap, he didn't yet know that Cincinnatus Leconte was promised a great destiny. He knew, however, that Joséphine—who spoiled him and whom he considered more like an aunt—would be instrumental in whatever success awaited her husband's career. The adults around him were heaping praise on Joséphine Laroche, who was then in her fifties. Everyone agreed that she was a "strong woman" who dispensed "very good advice" to her husband, especially because she closely followed politics.

In Joseph Laroche's family, there was another famous politician: his paternal uncle Tancrède Auguste.[64] In March 1896, Tancrède Auguste was appointed one of the five members of the State Secretaries Council, which served as an interim government after the sudden death of President Florvil Hyppolite before the end of his term. The interims lasted seven days, long enough for the deputies to elect the new head of state. But seven days is ample time to develop a taste for the presidential function, even when collectively assumed.

African slaves processing sugar cane on the Caribbean island of Hispaniola.
1595 engraving by Theodor de Bry.

The French exterminating the Black Army, during the Haitian War of
Independence. 1805 engraving.

Toussaint Louverture.

In August 1791, the slaves rebelled, soon joined by Toussaint Louverture, a fine strategist and a good cavalryman. He was born on a plantation near Le Cap in 1743. After having taught him to read and write, his master had freed him at thirty-three years old. Having become a landowner, Toussaint Louverture in turn owned slaves, which did not stop him from wanting to put an end to the system.

"I was born a slave, but nature gave me a soul of a free man...."
—Toussaint Louverture

Death of Toussaint Louverture (1843- 1803).

Born in slavery as the son of the African prince Gaou Guinou, Toussaint Louverture was Haiti's greatest warrior and one of its founding fathers. Born on a plantation near Le Cap, Toussaint Louverture was the first black general in the French army, the first black governor of a colony, and the "governor for life" of Haiti. Louverture freed the slaves of Haiti—in the only permanently successful slave revolt in history—and wrote the first constitution for Haiti. After paving the way for others to win the fight for freedom, Toussaint died in prison only six months before Haitian Independence Day. In Joseph Laroche's family, Toussaint Louverture was venerated because he embodied the Haitian fight for freedom.

"In overthrowing me, you have done no more than cut down the tree trunk of the Black Liberty in Saint-Domingue. [It] will spring back from the roots, for they are numerous and deep."

—Toussaint Louverture

In August 1912, Tancrède Auguste in turn acceded to the highest office. But Joseph was not around to congratulate him about it. The *Titanic* had sunk four months earlier.

. . .

Whether rich or poor, black or biracial, from the north or the south, Haitians are proud and dignified. They owe it to their past. They owe it to their enslaved ancestors who spilled their blood to break their chains and conquer their freedom. It is a precious legacy. They would not sell it off for anything in the world.

Euzélie Laroche was raised in this spirit, and Joseph noticed that any behavior not consistent with it deeply hurt his mother.

One evening, Joseph's mother came home as depressed as she'd been after the sinking of the *Ville de Saint-Nazaire*. Worried, Joseph pressed her with a thousand questions, but she only repeated, "I have never felt so humiliated in my whole life." Her eyes, void of their usual light, would not meet his, so Joseph decided to investigate, sending the maid for news the next day. With a hint of shame, she finally told Joseph about what was traumatizing his mother, as well as the whole country—an incident that had started with a commonplace arrest, 250 kilometers from the Laroche residence, on the road to Port-au-Prince.

In September of 1897, the police had stopped to question a coach driver as he was cleaning the car of his boss, Émile Lüders,[65] a businessman of black and white ancestry. When they accused the driver of theft, heated words were exchanged. When Lüders hurried over to assess the situation, he was accused of assault and later sentenced to one year of imprisonment.[66] Because Émile Lüders's father was German, however, this was enough for the German ambassador, Count Schwerin,[67] to intervene and demand his release as well as the removal of the judges and police officers involved in the case. The Americans also insisted that the Haitian government pardon Lüders, so it did, and the businessman sought shelter abroad.

In Germany, this diplomatic gesture was only half-pleasing, since the Haitian judges and policemen hadn't been dismissed as demanded. Two German warships were sent to Port-au-Prince right away, threatening to bomb the city if new requests were not satisfied within...four hours. Berlin demanded that Émile Lüders be allowed to return immediately to Haiti and be indemnified in the amount of twenty thousand dollars. The Haitian government was also to formally apologize to Germany, salute the German flag with twenty-one cannon shots, and host an official ceremony at the presidential palace in honor of Count Schwerin.

The people in Port-au-Prince rejected the ultimatum and declared themselves ready, if need be, for a mismatched battle against the Germans. However, President Tirésias Simon Sam[68] was not a man of honor and courage. He yielded and acceded to Berlin's demands. The people were outraged. They felt betrayed, ridiculed, and humiliated, just like Euzélie Laroche, who couldn't hide her dejection from her son. Euzélie felt all the more indignant because it was the second time Germany had attacked the nation's honor. Before that, in June 1872, Berlin had dispatched two warships[69] to Port-au-Prince to demand payment of three thousand sterling pounds from the Haitian government, accusing it of having allowed the shops of two German nationals to be ransacked. Without waiting for a reply, German Captain Karl Batsch[70] had seized two ships from the Haitian navy. Their backs to the wall, the authorities had to pay. But what a surprise when they got the two ships back! On both decks lay the Haitian flag, stained with excrement—an affront that aroused anger and indignation among the Haitian intellectuals, starting with "national poet" Oswald Durand,[71] cousin of the late writer Arnold Laroche, himself Joseph Laroche's cousin. He published a vengeful ode that made a splash. The last two lines were these irrevocable verses:

> *Heads up high and brave, we threw the money,*
> *as a bone is thrown to dogs!*

Two humiliations in a row for such a small country: it didn't take Joseph Laroche very long to understand that real life was nothing like the stories he'd been fed since childhood. It was not the shrewdest who got through, but rather the strongest and most violent.

■ ■ ■

Violence is endemic in Haiti, or *Ayiti*[72] (mountainous land), as it was called by the Native Americans "discovered" by Christopher Columbus in December 1492. They had greeted him with open arms...to their great misfortune. After the Genoese seafarer, others swarmed in quickly. They imposed their law, raped the women, and enslaved the men, forcing them to work in the gold mines. Following cruel mistreatment, murders, and epidemics, the Arawaks[73] were decimated. In 1492, there were one million Native Americans on the island. In 1550, only 150 were left.

In the meantime, the Spaniards imported slaves from Africa. In 1670, the French, who settled on the west side of the island, followed their lead. By 1791, the Saint-Domingue colony counted 455,000 blacks, thirty thousand free people of color, and twenty-eight thousand whites. The blacks slaved in the plantations; the whites—males and females—reaped the fruits and showed unbridled cruelty. The masters and their spouses often tortured and killed the slaves in cold blood.

"A young lady, one of the most beautiful women on the island, was having a formal dinner," Alexandre Wimpffen, chief of staff of the Austrian military recounts. "Furious because of a failed pastry dish, she ordered for the black cook to be seized and thrown into the burning oven." Wimpffen, who was passing through Saint-Domingue, was a guest at that dinner.

In response to all the cruelty, a revolt was brewing. Led by the free blacks and the freed slaves, it echoed the French revolution that had led to the decapitation of King Louis XIV in Paris.

When the biracial citizens of Saint-Domingue demanded weapons and the same rights as the white colonists, nobody listened. In February 1791, their leaders Vincent Ogé[74] and Jean-Baptiste Chavannes[75] were captured and decapitated in Le Cap. In August, the slaves rebelled, soon joined by

Toussaint Louverture, a fine strategist and a good cavalryman. He was born on a plantation near Le Cap in 1743. After having taught him to read and write, his master had freed him at thirty-three years old. Having become a landowner, Toussaint Louverture[76] in turn owned slaves, which did not stop him from wanting to put an end to the system.

On the insurgents' side, Toussaint Louverture first allied himself with the Spaniards against the French, and then with the latter against the former, after the proclamation in September 1793 of the abolition of slavery in Saint-Domingue by commissioners Sonthonax and Polverel, who had arrived from Paris. It was the beginning of a swift ascent for the former slave turned hero. The "Directory" appointed him brigadier general before entrusting him with command of the army. Toussaint Louverture then rapidly wove his web, eventually becoming the head of Saint-Domingue, having driven the English forces out of the island. On July 8, 1801, Toussaint Louverture appointed himself governor for life, two months after having promulgated an autonomous constitution that laid the foundations of a new government. "There cannot be slaves on this territory," article three of that text stipulated. "Any man, regardless of his color, is eligible for any job," article four added.

But in Paris, where power switched hands, Napoleon Bonaparte would have none of it. He sent a task force of thirty thousand men, commanded by his brother-in-law General Leclerc, to reinstate slavery. Betrayed, captured, deported, Toussaint Louverture died on April 7, 1803, in Fort-de-Joux[77] prison in the Doubs, France.

...

In 1802, the 9th year of the Haitian Independence Revolution, the French
landed a force of 16,000 soldiers led by Napoleon's brother-in-law,
General LeClerc.

Revenge taken by the Black Army for the cruelties of the French, 1802.

Old view of Fort de Joux, France. Created by Bocion,
published in *L'Illustration, Journal Universel*, Paris, 1860.

Located in the Jura mountains, near Switzerland, Fort-de-Joux was built in the twelfth century. Between 1678 and 1815, it became a state prison for domestic and foreign prisoners, including Toussaint Louverture, leader of Saint-Domingue's slave insurrection.

In Joseph Laroche's family, they honored Toussaint Louverture because he embodied the Haitian fight for freedom.

His uncle Arnold Laroche, the late poet, even paid him a beautiful tribute in a poem that became famous—a piece that, according to the Laroche family, Euzélie often read to her son. The poem begins as follows:

In a dark dungeon at the Joux fort, in France
Was languishing an old black man who had the universe's admiration
Betrayed by the French, jealous of his valor
The Black man was thrown in that fort with his feet in irons.
Scorning the atrocious cruelty of a consul
He kept repeating: "I die for my country!"
But one night, thinking of his homeland's sky,
Of his wife, his sons, his corn fields
The warrior exclaimed in a sincere accent:
"O my country! My heart filled with your sweet memories,
Can no longer moan in the strange land
The dungeon vault hears too many of my sighs.
That French general who is battling the world,
Does he know his prisoner's torments?
Alas! He has thrown me in this squalid pit!
Bonaparte, give me back my wife and children!"

Toussaint Louverture was no longer around to lead the fight, so Lieutenant Jean-Jacques Dessalines picked up the torch. He crushed the French army during a battle in the city of Vertières and proclaimed Haiti's independence on January 1, 1804. Cap Français was renamed Cap-Haïtien.

. . .

If today the Haitian national anthem, "La Dessalinienne,"[78] bears the name of the "Father of Independence," it was not always so. Indeed, during Joseph Laroche's youth, the anthem he proudly sang at school while saluting the flag every morning was called "When Our Ancestors Broke Their Shackles." Euzélie's son was probably glad to sing it, even more so because his cousin by marriage, the "national poet" Oswald Durand, ardent critic of the Germans, wrote the lyrics. The story of this anthem is, in fact, amusing. It was played for the first time in 1893, on the occasion of officially welcoming a...German ship, stopping over in Port-au-Prince:

> *Now to work, you descendants of Africa,*
> *Yellow and Black, sons from the same cradle*
> *The ancient Europe and the young America*
> *See us from afar and try the tough attack*
> *Let us plough the soil, which in the year 1804*
> *Our fathers conquered with strong arms*
> *Now it is our turn to fight*
> *With this cry: "Progress or death!"*

However, Oswald Durand's lyricism cannot erase Haitian history. On January 1, 1804, when independence was proclaimed, the general euphoria was contagious. It was short-lived, however, because the country was divided and hungry for revenge.

The new strongman, Jean-Jacques Dessalines, ordered the killing of the last French remaining on the island, with the notable exception of priests, physicians, and a few people favorable to the cause of the revolution. In Port-au-Prince, the massacre took place at the end of March. A witness, Samuel News, first mate on an American schooner, recalls that "the blacks went to the different houses inhabited by whites, knocked down the doors, dragged out the unfortunate victims found inside and, after having completely stripped them and left them naked, barbarically massacred them with sabers."

...

Portrait of Jean-Jacques Dessalines (1758-1806) on a Haitian banknote.

The gourde is the national currency of Haiti.

Jean-Jacques Dessalines.

Jean-Jacques Dessalines, (1758-1806), a leader of the Haitian Revolution and the first ruler of an independent Haiti, waving his sword and holding the head of a female French colonist.

Two years after being anointed emperor, Dessalines was murdered by his own "friends." His replacement sanctioned the partition between the north and the south, between the "negroes" and the biracials. The south was led by Alexandre Pétion,[79] who was biracial, and the north by a black president, Henri Christophe,[80] who would later have himself crowned king by a French archbishop. Joseph's grandfather, shoemaker Henri Laroche, attended the enthronement. He even sat in the first row because of his special relationship with Christophe, whom he'd known since the king was still only a president.

How did they know each other? Joseph wondered.

Lisettine shared the story with her grandson:

"Your grandfather was a good shoemaker, and his work was very much appreciated. The president eventually learned of it. One day, he had him called and requisitioned him immediately to make him his bootmaker. Can you imagine? Your grandfather was Christophe's personal bootmaker! Amazing! He fashioned the king's ankle boots as well as shoes for the soldiers of his army. It was a heavy responsibility. Your grandfather was torn between pride and fear in serving that man. As a matter of fact, the first time he appeared in front of Christophe, he was ill at ease. When your grandfather said his first name was also Henri, Christophe stared at him and said: 'Starting today your name is no longer Henri but "Cadet." ' This is how your grandfather ended up with this nickname. Since that day, people in Le Cap have been calling him 'Cadet' and he kept that name until his death."

Portrait of Alexandre Pétion (1770-1818) on a Haitian banknote.

Alexandre Pétion became the first president of the Republic of Haiti. He is one of Haiti's founding fathers, along with Toussaint Louverture, Jean-Jacques Dessalines, and Henri Christophe. The Port-au-Prince suburb Pétion-Ville is named in his honor. He was biracial, born in Haiti to a Haitian mulatto mother and a wealthy French father (who withheld his name because the child was too dark). The name Pétion came from the French-patois nickname Pichon, which means "my little one."

King Christophe was not loved by his subjects, but he did not care. He wanted to introduce them to modernity, regardless of the cost. He put into place a health service, codified the laws, founded a printing house, created an arts academy, distributed land to the soldiers, built several schools, and renamed the city Cap Henri. To an English visitor, Admiral Home Propalm, who pointed out to him that his subjects worked a lot more than in other places in the country, Christophe expounded his vision:

"You do not understand. You do not understand that my race is as old as yours. Except in Haiti, nowhere on the planet have the negroes been able to resist against you. Everywhere else we have become animals, and like cattle under the whip, we have submitted. Why is that? Because, sir, we lack pride, and we do not have pride because we do not have memories.

"Listen, sir, you are hearing the song of a drum. Somewhere, my people are dancing. This is all we have—the drum, laughter, dance, our love for each other and our courage—nothing that the white man can appreciate. Because you show contempt for our dreams, you kill our serpents and break our fetishes that you mistake for our gods.

"Maybe if we had something to show you, you would respect us, and if we had something to show ourselves, we would respect ourselves. But where are our great men? And if with our own hands we could touch things we created ourselves, towers, palaces, monuments, maybe we would find in them the certainty of our strength.

"During my whole life, be sure of it, I will work to build that pride that we so much need and I will build it in a way that it will be understood by both blacks and whites. I think of the future, sir, not the present. I will teach pride to my people, must I for that break their back with work."

Doggedly, Christophe had his people build a palace with 365 doors and a fortress equipped with 200 cannons at the top of a mountain that was practically inaccessible. He feared the return of the French and wanted to have the means to push them back in case of invasion. But at what cost? Thousands of men were mobilized by force to lift enormous blocks to the top. A lot of them died under the whip.

■ ■ ■

Portrait of Henri Christophe (1757 – 1820) on a Haitian banknote.

Henri Christophe was the sole monarch of the Kingdom of Haiti. Christophe was a former slave who rose to power in the ranks of the Haitian revolutionary military. After Dessalines was assassinated, Christophe created a separate government in the north of Haiti. He is known for constructing Citadel Henri (now known as Citadelle Laferrière), the Sans-Souci Palace, and numerous other palaces and fortresses, in the hopes it would make French incursion in the event of an attack less likely. In August of 1820, King Christophe suffered a stroke and became paralyzed. When his army abandoned him, he killed himself with a self-inflicted gunshot on October 8, 1820.

The Citadel, in Milot, Haiti.

The Citadel on a Haitian banknote.

King Christophe met a tragic end. First, his body betrayed him: a stroke paralyzed him. Then his army abandoned him, and when some of his men rose against him, revolt spread very rapidly. Unable to contain it, the king chose to commit suicide.

He shot himself in the head on October 8, 1820, only forty-six years before Joseph Laroche was born. In 1866, Cap Henri was once again Cap-Haïtien, but Christophe's reign still fueled conversations in town. His supporters praised the visionary builder, while his detractors evoked a tyrant. This debate shook the north, but also the entire country, soon reunified by Jean-Pierre Boyer.[81] The heated debate illustrated an important question for Haiti: how could its citizens reach equality when, from infancy, the nation had been fed with brutality? How can a country seek the light when all it had known was darkness?

Poet Aimé Césaire,[82] who dedicated a piece to Christophe, wrote that the fight for independence cost a lot of blood and tears. "It was a heroic act, but almost nothing compared to the issues it brought forth once independence was conquered. Only after independence did the real fight begin, with freedom taking on its full meaning. Only after independence did the great choices emerge: liberty, democracy, or autocracy. When one fights for himself, there is no more possible alibi. King Christophe was facing this new reality. He'd been a rebellious slave, a man of blood and pride, but despite his good intentions, he failed because he was not ready."

■ ■ ■

At fourteen, Joseph Laroche probably did not really care about Christophe, and whether his actions had been right or not.

All he wished for was to, one day, be able to tour the "Citadel," what Lisettine called the royal fortress. A lot of people in Le Cap talked about it but few dared venture

inside; they feared that the ghost of the monarch buried under the grass would lure them to his grave.

"It is far away, my little boy, far away!" Lissetine said. "From here, one must walk at least five good hours to get there. But you will see when you go one day: it is spectacular. The cannons are still there, intact, their bullets still lodged inside. When your grandfather wanted to see the king, he would go to the Sans Souci palace[83] instead. That is what Christophe called the castle, where he held big receptions. It is located at the foot of the Citadel. But today only ruins remain."

Lisettine explained to Joseph that the palace had been partly destroyed by the infamous earthquake of 1842. It had never been rebuilt. On the other hand, the Notre-Dame de l'Assomption du Cap cathedral, which had been completely flattened by this same earthquake, had been rebuilt. It was even more beautiful now and, whenever beauty was born from disaster, it prompted Lisettine to wonder, "Is it not proof that God is stronger than men?" In Joseph's mind, unfortunately, the earthquake was just one more catastrophe that he compared to the several shipwrecks that already disturbed him. "Is it worth it visiting a palace that did not withstand the fury of nature?" he asked himself, perplexed.

Like many children his age, Joseph Laroche would only become interested in this page of history much later. The same could be said for Luc Grimard,[84] the friend who'd had to withdraw from high school for family reasons.

■ ■ ■

After becoming a writer, Luc Grimard evoked King Christophe's splendor:

Sir, a hundred years ago, you lived in glory
Flags, soldiers, drums, the Queen and her ladies,
The golden stream that follows all Majesties—
All this existed only for your vanity,
Choking the peoples' freedom

From King Christophe's controversial legacy, Euzélie Laroche learned with certainty: education is a "miracle weapon" for those who want to develop their minds and their country; therefore, whenever parents can afford it, they should send their children to the best schools and push them to get as far as possible in their studies.

At the time, education was mainly Catholic, in keeping with the concordat signed between Haiti and the Vatican[85] in March of 1860. This agreement allowed the new state to normalize its relationship with the Church by financing the dispatching and salaries of missionaries. It also allowed Haiti to come out of its diplomatic isolation by obtaining the Holy See's acknowledgment that would be followed by the United States' two years later.

In 1872, the nuns of St. Joseph of Cluny[86] founded a religious school for girls in Le Cap. In 1878, the Brothers of Christian Instruction[87] opened a school for boys that welcomed eighty-eight children in its first year. Joseph Laroche would be educated there, learning from a curriculum based on the one used in European high schools, "with Latin and Greek in first place," as noted at the time by Belgian journalist Gustave de Molinari, who was passing through the island.

Other than these denominational schools, there was the Lycée National du Cap,[88] a renowned school whose principal, Joseph Augustin Guillaume, was Haitian. There were also several secondary schools opened by Martinicans or locals like Edmond Étienne, founder of Sainte-Marie School. Edmond Étienne had received higher education from the Jesuits in France. Back in the country in 1898, this "good Catholic" wanted to meet the "educational needs" of the population. When the school opened, it was an immediate success. Six years later, Le Cap's bishop, His Grace Kersuzan,[89] offered to take over. Edmond Étienne accepted and went back to being simply a teacher.

To Euzélie Laroche and the well-to-do families in Le Cap, Edmond Étienne was a model to follow. He had been in France, where he'd received several diplomas, and was brilliant. He was also a good Christian who'd remained obedient to his bishop; he was "malleable" and "regularly attended worship ceremonies," according to Gustave de Molinari.

Euzélie was dreaming of the same success for her son, especially now that Joseph knew what he wants to be: an engineer. "Why?" his mother asked, delighted, the first time he expressed his interest. "Why not?" Joseph had smiled, surprised by the question.

· · ·

Euzélie Laroche was proud of her son, who had an extraordinary faith. To encourage him on this path, she was ready for any sacrifice, any expense, as she proved for Joseph's First Communion. On that Sunday, she'd organized a great dinner. She had hosted family, friends, and neighbors. Everyone had drunk, eaten, danced to their heart's content. Euzélie had been pleasantly surprised to see her son execute a few steps of meringue and quadrille; she had complimented him, surprised that Joseph had kept his dancing skills hidden. As he gained more independence, he kept even more.

That Sunday, the Laroches were not the only ones celebrating, as First Communions were grand events in Le Cap. Men, women, and children paraded in beautiful outfits, and houses were spruced up for the feast that followed the rite of passage.

Within the families of those children who were to receive the holy sacrament, everyone was mobilized for the success of the grand parties, planning for any unforeseen situation. Historian Marc Péan explains that "formal invitations did not count. Any guest, whoever he or she was, was welcome. On those days, the streets of Le Cap were very animated. Groups were formed as people met and suddenly decided to go visit this or that family." The poor "had to borrow to cover the expenses arising from the occasion. Never mind that. It was essential to save face and, particularly, to correctly carry out one's role in these moments dedicated to opening one's doors to God's children."

God was everywhere in Le Cap—in the homes, in the schools, as well as in the city's hospice. The facility, kept by French nuns who cared for the sick and helped the poor while taking care of their own spiritual well-being, was overseen by His Grace Kersuzan, a Breton who had disembarked in Le Cap in 1883. He was strict and austere, but he had great influence on his followers, including the pious Euzélie Laroche, who had profound respect for him. As a matter of fact, when Euzélie sent Joseph to France in 1901, it was to this prelate that she entrusted her son.

As soon as he arrived in the country, His Grace Kersuzan did not hide his hostility against the competing religions. In November 1898, he launched an "anti-superstition" campaign with the ambition to fight Vodou, which he considers a barbarian fraud. With the support of the Haitian government, Kersuzan encouraged the population to "destroy as soon as possible all fetishes and superstition items." He believed that the world needed to be "civilized" by the Church, and that the infusion of the morality of the Gospels could only enhance the lives of Haitian citizens. He and his French peers considered Vodou[90] a kind of "homicidal magic" practiced by "demonic" beings that held "nocturnal orgies" in cemeteries.

Protestants[91] were also in the Church's line of fire because they embodied the American model rejected by France and its missionaries. Therefore, they also needed to convert and embrace Catholicism only.

Faced with the outcry caused by this crusade and the tensions it created, the Haitian government eventually backed out and pulled the support it was giving to the Church. However, the persecution was not cancelled, only postponed. A second anti-superstition campaign, even more virulent, would be launched in the country in 1911.

IV. Institution Du Saint-Esprit

Many times, Joseph Laroche wondered how it must feel to leave one's mother, one's island, and one's solid ground for the first time. He'd spent months preparing for the shock of separation—one he knew to be inescapable. Although he had planned for the best, imagined the most positive scenarios, shielding his mind from not-so-joyous prospects, he found himself heavy-hearted after boarding the ship heading to France. From the deck, he glimpsed his mother and grandmother shaking white handkerchiefs on the dock. He waved in return, recreating one of those farewell scenes he'd himself often witnessed as a young child, right here, at this same port. Before this day, he'd thought it an obsolete custom and, in fact, tacky: standing on the deck, however, he wished the moment would never end.

It hadn't been easy to bid adieu: to listen to his mother's last words of advice, and to hug the women, one last time. Tight-throated, he'd felt swollen with emotions. As he swallowed tears, he'd forced a smile and pretended to be fine.

And now, the liner was inexorably moving away. Soon, all that would remain of Euzélie and Lisettine would be two small dots in the horizon. Then, nothing. They would disappear—out of Joseph's sight.

A few weeks before, on his fifteenth birthday, Joseph promised himself that, as soon as he got to Le Havre, he'd buy the first newspaper he could find to send it to his mother for her to treasure. He imagined Euzélie as she turned the pages in front of her customers and commented on the articles about the great people of this world. She would tell them: "You see, this is the day my son arrived in France!"

As Joseph started a new chapter in his life, in 1901, the news reported the deaths of some famous people: on January 22, the Queen Victoria passed away in the United Kingdom, followed five days later by composer Giuseppe Verdi[92] in Italy. On September 9, painter Toulouse-Lautrec[93] died in France. His demise was followed by the murder, five days later, of American president William McKinley.[94]

• • •

66 That's all a man can hope for during his lifetime—to set an example—and when he is dead, to be an inspiration for history. 99
—William McKinley, 25th President of the United States

After the ship pulled away, it only took it a few minutes to reach the high seas. The time for crying was over: Joseph decided to pull himself together and embrace his new adventure. After all, he was not alone.

His mother had entrusted him to His Grace Kersuzan, who was traveling with him. The bishop of Le Cap was returning to France, as he regularly did within the scope of his duties.

Upon their arrival at Le Havre, Kersuzan would accompany Joseph by train to the city of Beauvais, in the north of France. Euzélie had enrolled her son at Institution du Saint-Esprit, a boarding school for boys kept by Spiritan fathers.

After having helped the young boy settle, Kersuzan would return to his native Brittany, a place he greatly missed whenever he went away. The bishop had come, once again, to recruit priests for Haiti, and Brittany was an inexhaustible pool. Since six pioneer clergymen from the area had left for Port-au-Prince in April of 1864, the pipeline had not run out, despite the threat of the yellow fever in Haiti, which was particularly deadly to non-natives every year. By 1896, within thirty years, 177 ecclesiastics among 272 had died and four bishops among seven.

Portrait of Queen Victoria

As Joseph started a new chapter in his life, in 1901, the news reported the deaths of some famous people: on January 22, the Queen Victoria passed away in the United Kingdom, followed five days later by composer Giuseppe Verdi in Italy.

Portrait of Giuseppe Fortunino Francesco Verdi.

Giuseppe Fortunino Francesco Verdi (1813–1901) was an Italian opera composer. He was born near Busseto to a family of moderate means and received a musical education with assistance from a local patron. By his thirties, he had become one of the pre-eminent opera composers in history. He also briefly served as an elected politician.

The Seated Clowness, **by Henri de Toulouse-Lautrec, French Post-Impressionist, 1896, lithograph.**

Toulouse-Lautrec loved a good party and was renowned for turning up at events in a fancy dress. As a big fan of absinthe, Toulouse-Lautrec decided to develop his own recipe for a cocktail containing the spirit. The drink was named 'Tremblement de Terre' or 'The Earthquake' because it was a strong mixture with cognac. He lived from 1864 to 1901.

Portrait of William McKinley (1843–1901).

William McKinley was the twenty-fifth president of the United States. According to the magazine *Mental Floss*, during a public reception on Sept. 6, 1901 at the Pan-American Exposition in Buffalo, NY, Leon Czolgosz shot McKinley twice in the torso while the president greeted guests in a receiving line. "McKinley allegedly uttered, 'Don't let them hurt him,' as the angry mob descended on Czolgosz. Later, at the Emergency Hospital on the Exposition grounds, McKinley said of his assassin, 'It must have been some poor misguided fellow,' and 'He didn't know, poor fellow, what he was doing. He couldn't have known.' "

Ministry in Haiti[95] was difficult, and not only because of the diseases; one had to spend days on horseback to reach the farmers on the heights: former slaves refusing to be agricultural workers had founded small operations in the hills. Until 1900, the priests survived for an average of three years. Kersuzan would return to visit the Saint-Jacques seminary, established in a castle that a rich, eccentric lady had bequeathed to him when he was staying with Nantes nuns in April of 1894. Since then, it had been in this vast domain, in the municipality of Guiclan, that Le Cap's bishop trained the priests he recruited. To all, Kersuzan invariably gave the same speech: he wanted "men" who were "ready to suffer and die" and not "little girls."

■ ■ ■

On the boat, His Grace Kersuzan was effusive about Brittany, and Joseph Laroche was not missing a word of his confidences. He was captivated, particularly because one of his ancestors was said to have come from the northwest of France. Under the black skin of the young Haitian flowed a bit of white blood. The idea made him smile: as he was a little bit French himself, he could already tell he'd feel at home in the country where he was headed.

The ship was gaining speed, and nothing could stop it anymore.

Joseph was amazed at it all: the great mast towers above, the shrouds that blew in the wind, and the boilers that roared. The hull cut through the foam: the machinery was perfectly oiled, the vessel held well at sea, and it was a beautiful sight.

The young Laroche was enthralled. He did not cease to admire everything happening around him. How does a liner float? He wondered. He remembered having asked that question in physics class. The teacher had then talked about Archimedes' principle, which stated that a body immersed in water received a vertical push from bottom to top, equal to the weight of the volume of liquid that had been displaced. Consequently, the bigger the ship, the more push it got, and the more it glided on the ocean.

Joseph was ebullient. From theory to practice, it was an occasion for him to review his knowledge and think about his mother. For the longest time, she had told him that it was the coffee from the Haitian farmers, sold on European markets, that allowed the country to stay afloat. For the first time, he was learning about the export process firsthand. In the hold of the ship, under his feet, the precious beans were stored. Several of these large bags, he knew, had been bought from Euzélie Laroche's Kay-Kafé. This made him proud.

It was already getting dark. After a quick meal, it was time for bed. In the small cabin that Joseph shared with His Grace Kersuzan, he recited his prayer and slid into his bunk, clutching between his fingers a small cross that his grandmother gave him. "With this, no harm will come to you or the ship," she had said. His first night on board indeed went very well.

The following days, on the other hand, were less exciting. Not only was Joseph bored, he was sea- and homesick. He wandered the boat aimlessly, feeling as if time were dragging. There was not much to see on the ocean. There was not much to do on the ship. Nowhere to run. No way to have fun. His Grace Kersuzan did nothing to amuse him. At fifty-three, Le Cap's bishop only cared for two things: praying and reading his bible. In a small yellow and black notebook, with a fountain pen—in style at the time—recently given to him by his mother, Joseph meticulously wrote about the days, and then the weeks, and eventually the months that passed. At the end of the eighty-third day, he was smiling. He was jubilant. Land was in sight. Finally, he was arriving. At last. The beginning of his new life.

• • •

The rest of the journey is easy. His Grace Kersuzan was in his element here in France; he gave orders and the luggage was immediately loaded en route to the train station. After a few hours of waiting, they at last departed for Paris, and then Beauvais.

Contrarily to Joseph Laroche's expectations, there was no culture shock. He had heard so much about France in Haiti, seen so many pictures of this country, crossed paths with so many French citizens at his mother's store, that he did not feel disoriented at all. The only thing that overwhelmed him that day, that made him feel elated, was the train. As he faced the majestic steel monster, his eyes opened wide.

Seated in the compartment next to the bishop, Joseph felt emotional. He thought again about a conversation he'd had with his mother, on the evening he had announced his intention to become an engineer. She had smiled with pride and had also whispered her approval in his ear: "That is good, son!" He had lowered his eyes in respect.

■ ■ ■

In Beauvais,[96] Joseph Laroche discovered his new school, where His Grace Kersuzan took him immediately. It was in a peaceful neighborhood, close to the train station and the old city ramparts. The huge building had multiple floors and it spread over several acres. There were trees everywhere.

"Bienvenue à l'Institution du Saint-Esprit!" a priest welcomed them warmly, opening the door wide.

As the luggage was unloaded, a few pleasantries were exchanged. Then, the tour began. First, they visited the high-ceilinged classrooms, which looked like the ones in Le Cap, only larger. The tables, in nine rows, occupied nearly the whole width of the oblong rooms. Each row seated six students. Three windows on each side allowed a brilliantly golden light to enter, and a crucifix hung on one of the walls.

The tour continued through the large refectory on the first floor, where the tables were arranged in three rows, two for the students and one for the teachers. They were long wooden tables that went from one end of the room to the other. At mealtimes, the teachers sat on chairs while the students sat on benches. From the corner of his eye, Joseph Laroche noticed another crucifix on the wall, along with two wooden statues of the Virgin Mary.

From *L'Illustration: Journal Universel*, Paris, 1868.

"The only thing that overwhelmed him that day, that made him feel elated, was the train. As he faced the majestic steel monster, his eyes opened wide."

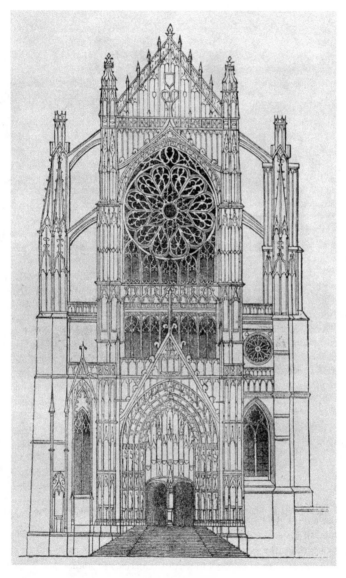

Beauvais Cathedral.

Beauvais Cathedral, side portal, old illustration. By unidentified author, published in *Magasin Pittoresque*, Paris, 1840.

Old house in Beauvais, France. Published in *Magasin Pittoresque*, Paris, 1840.

Beauvais is a city and commune in northern France. Joseph Laroche attended the Institut Agricole de Beauvais to begin training as an agronomic engineer. According to the *French Moments* website, one of the city's landmarks, the Beauvais Cathedral (which has been described as "ambitious and gravity-defying") boasts the record for the highest ceiling in a gothic choir. In fact, it was the tallest monument in the Christendom for four consecutive years until its lantern tower tragically collapsed.

He understood quickly that he would not come to this place only to feed his body but also to feed his soul, and the priest seemed to read the young man's mind: "Every student who enters the Institution du Saint-Esprit must comply to a very rigorous collective discipline.

For example, here in the refectory, silence is mandatory. A reader chosen among the children performs during the duration of the meal, with a certain number of readings reflecting our religious life."

The tour ended at the dormitory, a spacious room with fifty beds distributed in three rows, two against the walls and the third one in the middle. A quilt, almost half the size of the bed, was spread over the sheets, which were the same snowy white as the curtains. The room was bright, and the floor gleamed.

His Grace Kersuzan spent the night in Beauvais and left the next day. For the young Laroche, his last link to Haiti was broken. He was starting a new boarding school experience, far from his maternal cocoon.

■ ■ ■

Beauvais was a modest rural municipality, with twenty thousand inhabitants, almost twice the population of Le Cap. It was distinctly less sunny, as it was early fall, cold and foggy. Before the start of the school year, during specific hours, Joseph Laroche was allowed to leave the Institution du Saint-Esprit,[97] to explore his new living environment. He was accompanied by a Spiritan brother, a member of the school staff, and he awaited those excursions with excitement, like an explorer going on an adventure.

As he walked, Joseph discovered the city monuments: the royal factory renowned for its tapestries; the Hôtel-Dieu; the Saint-Pierre cathedral and its gothic architecture; the slaughterhouses of the Saint-Jacques neighborhood; the Gréber factory, famous for its ceramic; and the statue of local resistance fighter Jeanne Hachette, on the main plaza.

The story of this heroine who, weapons in hand, saved Beauvais by driving out the Duke of Burgundy's attacks in 1742, aroused Joseph's admiration.

She reminded him of a woman from his own country: Défilé the Madwoman,[98] who had lost her mind after witnessing the massacre of her brothers and children. Défilé the Madwoman became famous for saving Haiti's honor by herself, when everyone else failed to do so. In October 1806, Jean-Jacques Dessalines, the "Father of Haiti's Independence," was murdered in atrocious conditions: Soldiers cut his fingers to steal his valuable rings and stripped him from his rich clothing, before abandoning him to the crowd that stoned his body. When she discovered, horrified, the fate of the man who had sacrificed everything for the country's freedom, Défilé the Madwoman took action: she ran looking for a bag in which to put the bloody remains of the Emperor, which she took to the cemetery for a decent burial.

In front of Jeanne Hachette's statue, Joseph Laroche was enthralled. He dreamed of a similar monument for Défilé the Madwoman in Le Cap or in Port-au-Prince.

. . .

Another statue amazed Joseph that day, when his tour guide took him a little farther out, to Saint-Étienne. The church housed a representation of female Saint Wilgefortis. Perched next to a window with white panes, it was a rare piece, one of only two in France. The young Haitian was taken aback. St. Wilgefortis wore a…beard. *Sacrilège!* Who were those blasphemers who were defiling this sacred site? Where in the world was he? In Le Cap, such a heresy would have been impossible and, if it had happened anyway, His Grace Kersuzan would not have condoned it. Although his mother had him pray to many pious figures, he had never heard that one of the females had a beard.

Beauvais, France. Statue of Joanne Fourquet who was known as Joanne Hachette when she helped to prevent the capture of the town in 1456.

"What is this?" Joseph muttered under his breath. The Spiritan reassured him by telling what he knew of this story: "St. Wilgefortis was the Catholic daughter of a pagan king in Portugal. Despite her chastity vow, her father wanted to marry her to a Sicilian king, who had defeated him, in exchange for peace. So, Wilgefortis begged God to make her ugly. The miracle happened: she grew a beard. Disgusted, her suitor was driven away. The outraged father had St. Wilgefortis crucified."

. . .

Before setting foot in France, Joseph Laroche had seen pictures of Saint-Nazaire, Bordeaux, and, of course, Paris. He had been told, at great length, about the Eiffel Tower, the Notre-Dame Cathedral, and even the Seine. He knew all these places without having ever seen them. As a matter of fact, when he had arrived in Le Havre the other day, disembarking with His Grace Kersuzan at the Saint-Lazare, he had not felt too disoriented. Admittedly, the enormity of the place and the frenetic traffic around the Cour de Rome had impressed him. But his uncle, Nemours Auguste, had talked about it for so long and in such minute detail that he had not been surprised. In the carriage taking him to the station for the train to Beauvais, in the north, he had in fact enjoyed announcing to the bishop the names of the great boulevards that the coach driver and his horse would take. He had been wrong only once, but the clergyman had been impressed by the young man's memory.

While Le Havre and Paris didn't surprise him, Beauvais looked nothing like what Joseph Laroche had imagined. It constituted a facet of France he hadn't been prepared for, and it surprised Joseph day after day. At first, he was intrigued by the clogs some of the passersby wore, coming home from the factory or the fields; the clogs clacked loudly on the sidewalk. Weird shoes, Joseph thought, wondering if, just like in Le Cap, the workers and farmers were the one who sustained the country. Just like in Le Cap, the streets were not very wide, the houses were not very tall, and the shops were not very big. Joseph almost expected to find a Le Cap newspaper at the stationery shop across the street—or even a sweet potato cake at the neighboring bakery. He imagined his mother's coffee shop around the corner. As he strode through the town, Joseph started feeling at home in his new space.

"Why Beauvais?" Joseph had asked his mother when she revealed his final destination.

"Because that town is of human size," she had replied. Furthermore, she'd explained, the Brothers of Christian Instruction, with whom Joseph was educated in Le Cap, thought very highly of it. As a matter of fact, they had taken all the necessary steps for Euzélie.

To tell the truth, Joseph would have preferred landing in Paris, like most of the Haitian students of the time, particularly as two of his uncles were established there. Being educated so close to family would have consoled him whenever homesickness struck. In addition, it so happened that one of his uncles, Jean-Baptiste Déjoie Laroche,[99] was a physician. In a country where winter often welcomed newcomers by giving them a bad cold, that could have been useful.

Whenever he thought about that uncle and all the others, Joseph felt perplexed, though. He did not understand why they all caught the same disease. Despite their comfortable situation in their respective fields, they all dreamed of only one thing: becoming President of the Republic of Haiti.

On his father's side, there was interim Tancrède Auguste, who would in fact become Haiti's ruler. On his mother's side, there was the ambitious Cincinnatus Leconte, who would also ascend to power. Also on his mother's side: the military man François Beaufossé Laroche and the doctor Jean-Baptiste Déjoie Laroche.

Cincinnatus Leconte.

On January 8th, 1908, President Nord Alexis was overthrown by putschist Antoine Simon. He was forced to exile, just like his Minister of Interior who was no other than Cincinnatus Leconte, the husband of Joséphine Laroche, Joseph's dear cousin.

Jean-Jacques Dessalines Michel Cincinnatus Leconte (1854–1912) was President of Haiti from August 15, 1911 until his death on August 8, 1912. He was the great-grandson of Jean-Jacques Dessalines—a leader of the Haitian Revolution and the first ruler of an independent Haiti. Joseph Laroche was Leconte's nephew. A lawyer by trade, Leconte was forced into exile after a 1908 coup deposed of President Pierre Nord Alexis, the Haitian president under whom Leconte served as minister of the interior. Leconte led a successful rebellion from exile in 1911 and was unanimously elected President of Haiti by Congress on August 14, 1911. Leconte was killed in a mysterious explosion at the presidential palace in Port-au-Prince in August of 1912, just months after his nephew perished in the sinking of the *Titanic*.

The latter case was a bit more complex. Jean-Baptiste Déjoie Laroche had been raised and educated in Paris before returning to Le Cap with his medical diploma. He'd opened several drugstores, but none of them thrived, as the people were not used to "scientific medicine." Haitians preferred their good old traditional remedies, which were also cheaper. In addition, the power in place took offense at Jean-Baptiste Déjoie Laroche's overzealous entrepreneurship, which forced the doctor to leave Le Cap for Paris until 1912, the same year Joseph Laroche himself decided to return to the homeland. Jean-Baptiste Déjoie Laroche would then launch himself into politics and become a presidential candidate ten years later—without much success.

·· ·

Ding-dong! Ding-dong! The school bell was ringing, and Joseph Laroche was ready for the hard work that awaited him. On the first day, the students lined up in rows in the yard, in perfect order—all in navy-blue jackets that bore the Institution du Saint-Esprit insignia, pants and vest of the same color, tasseled cap, black silk tie, black shoes and white gloves. Joseph Laroche, attentive and focused, looked spic-and-span in the new jacket with a velvet collar and golden buttons. Not a movement in the line. Not a word. And certainly not a laugh. Right after roll call, the students walked to class in single file behind the impassive teacher, looking at each other from the corners of their eyes, smiling discreetly, making first contact from a distance, hoping a glance might lead to a beginning of a friendship later on the playground.

A lot of the customs in Beauvais felt familiar to Joseph. In fact, the only obvious difference between Institution du Saint-Esprit and Joseph's school in Haiti was that almost all the students in Beauvais were white, a fact that did not bother the mild-mannered young man. All secondary-school students in the world were the same, he figured. When they were not buried in their books and notebooks, and even when they were, they only thought about two things: marbles and girls. Only the setting was different. In fact, during the following days, Joseph would not take long to learn that, in addition to marbles, French children had many other games in common with Haitian kids: the boys in Beauvais also played dodgeball[100] and spinning top,[101] while the girls from the Saint-Joseph de Cluny school next door played hopscotch[102] and skipped rope.[103]

During recess, Joseph Laroche was the object of blatant curiosity. Imagine! A black student in a small rural municipality like Beauvais. That was unprecedented. When he'd arrived a few days before and was seen walking in town with his Spiritan guide, many had already wondered about him. And now he was to answer questions.

"Where is that?" an older student asked when he couldn't locate Haiti on the world map. He got four magic words for an answer: freebooters, pirates, ships, Caribbean. He finally found the island. The others too. Their eyes shone.

"How can you speak French like us?" The question asked by a big, freckled kid surprised Joseph. Must I tell the truth? he wondered. Tell them that their ancestors had enslaved his, forcing them to learn the masters' language, so that they could obey orders? If he told them, would they not be tempted later to show some kind of superiority toward him? After much hesitation, he finally chose a half-truth. "In Haiti the government encourages learning French in school because our two countries trade with each other," Joseph said.

"Why are you black?" a redhead then asked. Immediately, laughter burst out from everywhere as everyone had been dying to ask the same question. This time, however, Joseph Laroche felt even more embarrassed. He did not really know what to say, because he simply had never thought about it. He remembered wondering about race, long ago, when French and German customers came to his mother's Kay-Kafé. "Mom, they are white!" he had said, surprised. He could understand being the object of curiosity. Fortunately, the bells rang and freed him.

. . .

The Beauvais secondary school did not hide the fact that it "only catered to the elite." It welcomed about a hundred pupils, from "lower grades" to high school. It was administered by a father superior, assisted by a headmaster and a discipline master. The headmaster was responsible for anything related to instruction, while the discipline master was in charge of the students' health and behavior. While the teachers, mainly priests and brothers from the Saint-Esprit Congregation, followed the official curriculum, they ensured a "Christian and patriotic" education for the children. In 1901, the school included fifteen fathers, four scholastics (seminarians serving as supervisors or masters of students), seven brothers and the *agrégé* (certified master teacher). Among these teachers, one, considered a success story, had a name that was easy to remember: Beauvais, like the town. After attending Institution du Saint-Esprit as a student, Father Charles Beauvais[104] became the natural science, physics, and history teacher at the school, to the great delight of Joseph and his schoolmates.

"His students came to class as if it were a party," a teacher recounted, describing the atmosphere he created. "The reflections and stories, which were his specialties, chased away boredom and sharpened their desire for knowledge and learning."

But not all teachers were as popular. The homeroom teacher of the junior grade, Father Allheilig, was "the object of unanimous complaints from the students and the families," because he was "very unlikeable," with "his unpolished appearance, his provocative manners," and "his notorious incompetence." Another one of Joseph Laroche's teachers, Father Bécue, was also criticized in the same kind of language by the superior and by his own colleagues, who were annoyed by his lack of authority. Father Heitz, the head of the school since October 1900, lamented Bécue's leniency in these terms: "This year, the class was well balanced: apart from one scatterbrain, there were only placid, docile, hard-working children. He still could not control them. There was practically no progress and these kids are indiscriminately saying that they do nothing. They make a racket. While the teacher is meticulous, he's also a drag." This statement was echoed by those of the teachers: "They must transfer him if they care about learning, discipline and the good name of the house," the teachers wrote.

At Institution du Saint-Esprit, two-thirds of the students were boarders. They were entrusted to the school by families from the area as well as from Paris and its surroundings.

In addition to these French students, there were a few foreign boarders, children from well-to-do backgrounds, with parents who served as ministers, diplomats, or senior officials in their home countries.

These foreign students came from the West Indies, Africa, or Asia, where the Congregation of Saint-Esprit had missionaries or correspondents. "The Saint-Esprit school of Beauvais received two Chinese pagans. One of them converted after a year," pointed out Paul Lahargou, a member of the Catholic order.

The annual cost of boarding was one thousand francs,[105] payable in three installments—a huge amount in those times, particularly for the parents of students coming from very far away, like Joseph Laroche. In addition to this tuition, it cost eighty francs for the laundering and mending of linen, ten francs for the repairing of clothes and shoes, and twenty francs for a complete set of bedding. Piano, gymnastics, or fencing lessons included supplementary fees that ranged from two to ten francs.

Whether French or foreign, the boarders lived in community with constant supervision inside the walls of Institution du Saint-Esprit, including during short and long holidays. Except for a few students, Joseph and his schoolmates would spend all their school years there without returning to their families.

This did not bother the young Haitian. He'd prepared for his new life. From now on, his priority was to focus on his studies in order to keep the promise he'd made to his mother when leaving Le Cap: he'd get his baccalaureate and enter an engineering school so he could obtain the degree he aspired to. To get there, Joseph would not neglect any subject, be it those in which he excelled, such as mathematics, physics, and chemistry, or those in which he struggled, such as English. Joseph also wanted to make sure he succeeded in French, history, and geography. So, the first year in Beauvais, Joseph was attentive and participated in class. During study hours, he reviewed the subjects of the day, learned the lessons for the next day, and sometimes even got ahead by exploring the upcoming curriculum. He crammed so much that sometimes he forgot the noise of the outside world and the pains faced by French society.

But, in 1901, it was impossible to escape the news of the Dreyfus affair,[106] which continued to divide supporters and opponents of the Alsatian Jewish officer who, seven years earlier, had been sentenced to labor camp for life; the officer was accused of treason for the benefit of Germany, and he was deported to Devil's Island.[107] Although Joseph did not take part in the debate, he was not surprised to learn that the Catholic Church was anti-Dreyfus.

Back in Haiti, the missionaries had adopted a shocking attitude toward the Jews.[108] An article of the time, published in the Haitian newspaper *Le Nouvelliste,* reported that cloth mannequins had been paraded during Easter in a demonstration of anti-Semitism event: "Just as the bells rang to announce the glorious resurrection of the Christ, the mannequins that personify the Jews who crucified the Lord were assaulted with sticks. Next, they were set on fire and dragged through the city, still being beaten, until there was nothing left but a few shreds, burnt to ashes."

In France, against a backdrop of anti-Semitism, the Catholic Church and the military shared a common cause: the Dreyfus affair. The cause, however, had recently lost its greatest support at the highest level of the government, when the President of the Republic, Félix Faure,[109] passed away abruptly in January 1899. Since then, under the yoke of Faure's successor, Émile Loubet,[110] the new president of the Council, Waldeck-Rousseau,[111] a liberal and a republican, has been thoroughly clearing out: purging the administration, cleansing justice, cleaning up the army, and replacing prefects, judges, and military high officers. In August 1899, a review of Dreyfus' trial was conducted, and it was found that the War Council had sentenced the Alsatian captain to ten years of imprisonment despite all extenuating circumstances. Waldeck-Rousseau went out of his way to obtain a presidential pardon for him. Dreyfus was freed but not cleared. A long battle began for his exoneration. It would last six years.

Courtroom scene of the espionage trail of Captain Alfred Dreyfus at Rennes in 1899. Uniformed Dreyfus stands in the center background with artists and journalists in the left foreground.

A stamp printed in France circa 2006 shows reinstatement of Captain Alfred Dreyfus.

The Dreyfus Affair was a political scandal that erupted in France in 1896 and saw its resolution in 1904. It has become a notable example of a miscarriage of justice and exposed antisemitism within the French political system and army. The scandal began when in December 1894 Captain Alfred Dreyfus, a young Alsatian French artillery officer of Jewish descent, was sentenced to life imprisonment on Devil's Island for allegedly providing the German Embassy in Paris with French military secrets. After five years on Devil's Island, Captain Dreyfus was retried and found guilty in 1899. He was ultimately exonerated and released in 1906 when police discovered that another French officer was the real culprit. Dreyfus returned to the French Army and served the entirety of World War I, eventually being promoted to Lieutenant Colonel. Dreyfus died in 1935.

In June 1901, Waldeck-Rousseau attacked the clergy, irritated by its stance in the Dreyfus affair and its interference in political spheres. He passed the notorious Law of Associations[112] and suppressed nearly all of the religious orders in France. From now on, only authorized or recognized congregations could continue working in the field of education. Since approval was not easy to obtain, many members of the clergy eventually left France or entered civilian life. The Catholic Church was hit in the heart, especially as the Law on Associations followed severe 1881 and 1882 "anticlerical" legislation, which had triggered a general outcry in Beauvais by imposing secular education. The bishop himself, His Grace Péronne, had organized the resistance. It had led to the opening of Institution du Saint-Esprit, the school that welcomed Joseph Laroche. "His Grace Péronne insists on the necessity of founding this school to prevent the youth of the diocese from getting lost by going to the one in the city," Father Kieffer, the first superior of the school, reported. Only ten students enrolled at the beginning of its first school year in October 1889.

The bishop's public attacks had prompted the radicalization of the community which had, in reprisal, changed the names of the streets to secular ones, prohibited public processions and created the newspaper *La République de l'Oise* to counter *Le Moniteur de l'Oise,* which followed the agenda of the bishopric.

These tensions between clergy and public powers worried Joseph Laroche. What if the school did not obtain approval to continue its mission? What if it had to close its doors? What would become of the students, especially himself, the Haitian foreigner?

Who would care about him? Would he find himself on the streets? If yes, this meant he would not be able to take the *baccalauréat* exam and apply to a great engineering school. If his mother were here, he thought, or if only he had stayed home in Haiti, she could have at least taken matters into her hands. This would not be happening. In Haiti, she knew practically everyone, and there were well-placed people in the family. If things were not going well in Le Cap, she could send him to Port-au-Prince; if things were not going well in Port-au-Prince, she could dispatch him to Gonaïves or Les Cayes. There was always a way to sort out things in a small country like his. There always was a back-up solution, especially for people with money like his mother.

But here?

Powerless in those circumstances, Joseph shook his head to reassure himself, thinking that the situation would certainly improve because "God was watching." So, he might as well concentrate on his objective. Two months after the start of the school year, his grades were good. All that was left for him to do was prepare to face his first winter. It would be hard, and Joseph knew it, although he had everything he needed to protect himself, from a turtle-neck sweater to warm gloves to a lined coat. He already had a hard time enduring the harshness of fall, however. How would it be in a month? The only thing he liked in the season was the falling of yellow leaves. It was a beautiful sight, but it did nothing to warm him up.

■ ■ ■

At Institution du Saint-Esprit, the days were synchronized like music sheets. For Joseph, mornings were the most challenging. The bells rang at 5:00 a.m., waking him up in the impersonal dormitory. After washing rapidly in cold water, the students hurried to prayer at 5:20 a.m. in a brand-new chapel, inaugurated the previous February, the construction of which had been financed by the students' families and generous donors. At 5:30, the marathon resumed, with everyone going to study hall to study from their books and notebooks. Breakfast was at 7:15, before a visit with the physician, who was joined by the dentist on Tuesdays, and the barber on Tuesdays and Fridays. At 8:00, classes began. The schedule was immutable: a first recess at 10:00, then a second one after lunch and a last one after the 4:30 p.m. snack; study at 10:15 a.m., 1:30 p.m., and 5:15 p.m.; rosary at 5:00 p.m.; evening prayer at 7:00 p.m., before dinner, and then at 7:30 p.m., before bed.

Thursdays and Sundays were rest days. There was no class, but the boarders woke up at the usual time to maintain the daily rhythm. These days were partly spent in a country house, a magnificent twenty-five-acre property, that the school leased from the old Saint-Lucien abbey at the entry to the city. The students went on foot. They had lunch on site and played educational games. On Thursdays, they had composition in the morning and hiking in the afternoon. On Sundays, they went to two masses, at 6:30 a.m. and 8:30 a.m., and for another walk at 1:30 p.m.

During the first three months, Joseph Laroche followed the general rhythm with enthusiasm. By December, however, he couldn't help feeling homesick. It was his first Christmas away from Le Cap, and he loved the special way they celebrated this holiday at home. He loved the midnight mass, the nativity scene, as well as those hymns heard all over the city: *Please promptly get up, my neighbor. The Savior of the earth is among us, my neighbor.* Guessing his sadness, Euzélie wrote him a beautiful letter a few days before, to remind him of her affection and give him news of the family. So that he could feel included in the celebration, she sent him an article of the *Novateur*,[113] a newspaper in Le Cap describing the evening of December 24, 1901. When he received it a few weeks later, Joseph couldn't help crying. "As early as six o'clock in the evening," the article read, "the illuminated city of Carénage à la Fossette, from Petite Guinée to Bord de Mer, was already announcing the magnificence of the celebration. Cardboard lanterns were decorated with all kinds of drawings through which you could see the light of the reflecting candles. Men, women, and children carried paper lanterns and tallow candles attached to the end of sticks, this eager crowd avid for solemnity."

Poor Joseph. So many memories flooded his thoughts. He missed his mother. He missed Lisettine and all her stories—stories even more real than the history lessons at school, because his grandmother brought them to life. She had witnessed her time in history and knew how to create suspense when she described Haiti's past, or the anecdotes of his grandfather Henri Laroche's life. In fact, whenever she felt Joseph's captivation, Lisettine would pause, feigning fatigue. She took a deep breath to prolong the torture, and drank a little glass of rum before resuming her tale. Hanging on every word, the child would listen without a word. Attentive. Focused. Serious. Astounded.

How does one fight nostalgia? It was overcoming Joseph. He remembered scenes of his childhood, his city. It was as if he were there right now.

He remembered the narrow streets in Le Cap, the colorful houses, the sea and the sun, the beach in Labadie.[114] **Images of the Notre-Dame plaza, the Clugny market,**[115] **and even the fountain at the corner of Rue Royale and Rue du Conseil haunted him.**

And what could he do? Not much, unfortunately. The young Laroche felt powerless, especially because Christmas was not the only holiday he was deprived of. He was also missing, for the first time, New Year's Eve in Le Cap and, for Haitians, regardless of age, January 1 was sacred. It was not merely, like most places in the world, the end of a year and the beginning of another. It was also Independence Day with its immutable traditions, culinary and other. Haitians enjoyed a good soup made of squash,[116] the equivalent of the French pumpkin. At night they set off big firecrackers bought from the corner drugstore. It was a unique, liberating day that was lived fully. Afterwards, they waited until Carnival, two months later, to have fun again.

The only time Joseph had not celebrated Independence Day was in 1897. Poor Marie-Joseph, the wife of his uncle Edgard Laroche, had died on that very day, at only twenty-eight years old. So, the family had been in mourning while the whole city was enjoying the day wholeheartedly. Then, in February, Aunt Élide Laroche had passed away. Later, in August, Uncle Bertrand had committed suicide. In short, three deaths in eight months: that was a first for the Laroches. Maybe missing a national holiday brought bad luck, Joseph thought as he reminisced. Ah, nostalgia! It was like squash soup. You swallowed it rapidly, before moving to the next dish. That also, Joseph understood quickly. You do not feel sorry for yourself when you have your eyes set on a diploma. He couldn't go home anyway: not only was it expensive, the journey was too lengthy—he would have barely left in July and it would be time to be back for the new school year. So, at the start of 1902, Joseph Laroche immersed himself in his precious studies and in the school routine.

That year, the boarders and day pupils complained in the refectory, because they found the meals less appealing than usual. Sister Priscillien, the chef, had become sick and was not replaced; the father treasurer thought Sister Saint-Savin could take over the cooking, but she was not in good health, either, and was not cut out to lead a team anyway. The mother general of the sisters of Saint-Joseph de Cluny had promised to do her best to solve the problem, but the candidates were not exactly lining up.

Out of desperation, Institution du Saint-Esprit was considering calling on a cleaning lady to fill the position. "But we must be able to ensure this woman a stable situation until at least the end of the year," the superior wrote to management in Paris. "What do you think?"

Like the previous ones, the winter of 1902 brought days of "bad weather" and many cases of influenza. Many students were affected, beginning with Joseph Laroche. But, this time, the superior found an effective "remedy" to treat the sick. "I have them get coffee after dinner," he was pleased to say. This delighted the young Haitian, who thought of his mother with each sip in the cold winter that did not run out of drama: in March, a fourteen-year-old student contracted scarlet fever, raising concern in the school community, particularly as "the doctor did not find it necessary to send him to his family." The superior took a radical measure. He quarantined the boy above the nurse's office, with a nun beside him.

• • •

While Joseph Laroche got into the flow at his school in Beauvais, he still watched what was happening in his country and the neighboring islands, thanks to the Spiritans deployed at the school. They provided news in real time from their headquarters in France, which relayed the news to its different antennas in the provinces—many of the accounts inflicting great anguish on Joseph. At the morning service of May 9, 1902, he turned pale when the priest asked with a sad voice that they all pray for thirteen

Spiritans and "thousands of brothers and sisters in Martinique" who'd perished the day before, when Mount Pelée,[117] the old volcano in the city of Saint-Pierre, had erupted.

The horrifying tragedy reminded Joseph of the sinking of the liner *Ville de Saint-Nazaire*, of which he had also learned at mass. He thought about the victims, about the closeness Haitian people felt to their Martinican neighbors, whom they considered like brothers.

In fact, when Jean-Jacques Dessalines gained independence for his people in 1804, his thoughts went out to those nearby, who were still enslaved. "Unfortunate Martinicans," he exclaimed, "I wish I could fly to your help and break your chains. Alas! An invincible obstacle is between us. But maybe a spark from the fire that set us ablaze will spring from your soul!"

The awakening of Mount Pelée distressed Joseph even more when he remembered one of his grandmother's stories, about a great American traveler named John Candler.[118] When he arrived in Le Cap, shortly before the earthquake of 1842, Chandler had been said to be shocked by how the city "looked like Saint-Pierre in Martinique." Lisettine did not know Saint-Pierre or Martinique, but the comparison had had a big effect on her, and she had not failed to mention Pierre Chandler among the characters of the stories she told her grandson. The description seemed as real as the old iron box that allowed her to make a living as an ironer, and the memory of this detail worried Joseph today, as everything became confusing. He thought about his mother. What if she were in danger? True, there was no volcano in Le Cap. But what if an eruption in Saint-Pierre was to cause an earthquake in its twin city Le Cap? Shaking and miserable, Joseph Laroche asked for permission to call his mother. He was obtaining this exceptional favor the second time, after the call he'd made last September to say that he had safely arrived. It was such a relief to hear Euzélie's warm voice at the other end of the line.

But a few days later, Joseph relapsed, dismayed to learn from a Spiritan father that Haiti was once again in turmoil. President Tirésias Simon Sam, the same one who had angered Euzélie for having conspired with the Germans, finished his term in total chaos. On May 12, 1902, as he was announcing his resignation, shooting broke out in the Parliament. Panic ensued, and gunfire was also heard around Port-au-Prince. Violence rocked the county, and the state of affairs depressed Joseph, who felt completely powerless when he discovered the details of this violence. "The minor seminary received a good number of stray bullets," a Spiritan father reported. "It served as shelter for over four hundred people, including senators and deputies and their families. President Sam himself entrusted to our fathers three of his sons, deputies of the people, and some of his friends."

The next day, Tirésias Simon Sam fled the country, embarking for Paris with his family. The disastrous end of this Haitian presidency worried Joseph Laroche, particularly as he waited a long time before receiving reassuring news of his dear cousin Joséphine Laroche and her husband Cincinnatus Leconte. The latter was close to Tirésias Simon Sam, who had even chosen him to replace him as the head of the country. But, outraged, the population of Port-au-Prince, under a revolutionary committee, opposed the choice, preferring an interim government.

* * *

Regardless of what was happening in Port-au-Prince, in Le Cap, and in Haiti, Joseph Laroche had to pull himself together because another ordeal, more immediate, more personal, was waiting for him: the end-of-year exam, which included every single subject. It went from 8:00 a.m. to 6:00 p.m. with pauses for the 10:30 recess, lunch at noon, and the 4:00 p.m. snack. On that day, some students often quit, or were held back a year.

Thankfully, Joseph Laroche did not fail. He successfully passed this last stage and could attend with a smile his first prize-giving ceremony in Beauvais. The early celebration, which took place in July, was attended by the diocese, the priests, and the students' families. The guests were welcomed by the happy tunes played by the student brass band. At 1:45

p.m., the recipients lined up to receive the honors they deserved. Then, a talent show began, with elegantly crafted performances by the students, presented to a captivated audience for nearly two hours. It was a beautiful party, the last party the students would attend together before the summer break—an unforgettable moment for Joseph Laroche, who wished Euzélie were present to show the great pride she felt for her son.

V. Bread and Games

In July 1902, school was out of session for everyone, except for Joseph Laroche and the French boarders who remained on the premises. They woke up and went to bed at the same times as usual. They attended study hall, just as they did during the school year, and recited, even during vacation, the same number of prayers. The only difference was that the group traveled more often to the Saint-Lucien abbey, which had become its base camp, and they regularly went on excursions with the priests and brothers. Joseph discovered France through the Picardy region, instead of in books with black and white pictures. He explored a variety of scenery, plains, forests, and woods, of ponds, limestone hills, and smooth pebbles. He watched the harbor seals of Somme Bay and the avocets of Marais d'Isle. He visited Soissons, home of a legendary vase, as well as Noyon, where Charlemagne was made king.

Of all these trips, the one that left the deepest impression on him was the tour of Villers-Cotterêts, where famous writer Alexandre Dumas,[119] "the most Haitian of the French," was born in July 1802, on the first floor of a big house, in a room opening to the garden.

Dumas's father was born in Saint-Domingue from an enslaved black mother and a penniless colonist. He had made a career in the army and climbed the ladder to become the impetuous General Dumas, known for his military campaigns in Vendée, Italy, and Egypt. Upon his return to France in 1801, General Dumas was "ill, without employment, but happy to be reunited with his wife, whom he had missed a lot during this separation," Marcel Frossard, a pharmacist in Villers-Cotterêts and close friend of the Dumas family, shared. "So, what was bound to happen, happened: a happy family event came into preparation."

Portrait of Alexandre Dumas.

Born Dumas Davy de la Pailleterie (1802–1870) in Saint-Domingue, prolific French writer Alexandre Dumas was the grandson of Marie-Cessette Dumas, a black Haitian slave, and Alexandre Antoine Davy de la Pailleterie, an impoverished French nobleman. He is one of the most well-read French novelists whose works include *The Count of Monte Cristo, The Three Musketeers, Twenty Years After*, and *The Vicomte of Bragelonne: Ten Years Later*. He was called "the most Haitian of the French."

Alexandre Dumas leaving Marseilles aboard the yacht Montecristo. Published in *L'Illustration: Journal Universel*, Paris, 1860

Valley Puys, view from the garden of Alexandre Dumas.
From *Journal des Voyages* (1879-80).

In Le Cap, Euzélie also harbored great admiration for Alexandre Dumas. She knew some of his works, starting with *The Count of Monte-Cristo*. At home, she often delivered monologues from the writer, like this one, which Joseph never forgot: *I was born in Villers-Cotterêts, a small town in the department of Aisne, situated on the road between Paris and Laon, about two hundred paces from Rue de la Noue, where Demoustiers died, two leagues from Ferté-Milon, where Racine was born, and seven leagues from Château-Thierry, the birthplace of La Fontaine.*

Since his case of the blues at Christmas, Joseph Laroche no longer indulged in nostalgia or oversensitivity. But here, in front of the house where his "compatriot" was born, he couldn't help it. He was deeply moved. It was gut-wrenching. He felt it everywhere. He wished so much that he could share his joy right now, go home to Le Cap, and nestle into his mother's arms. But, deep down, he knew that the political climate had become particularly dire—dangerous—in Haiti. Since President Tirésias Simon Sam's turbulent departure, it had been total confusion. The country was on the verge of chaos, and Le Cap was falling apart, the scene of a fight between two former allies turned warring brothers: General Nord Alexis,[120] a leader of the opposition who had been imprisoned multiple times, and Anténor Firmin, the former Minister of Finance, who had destroyed the expensive railway project brought forth by Dr. Nemours Auguste, Joseph Laroche's uncle.

Following President Tirésias Simon Sam's turbulent resignation, an interim government had been put in place to deal with day-to-day matters, before a new head of state was appointed. Anténor Firmin refused to be part of it, contrarily to General Nord Alexis, in whom he had complete trust. Freed from daily management, Anténor Firmin wanted in fact to prepare his candidacy for the presidential election. He had a good chance. The thing was, General Nord Alexis also had great ambition. Supported by the interim government, he turned against Anténor Firmin and triggered a bloody civil war. Anténor Firmin's house in Le Cap was ransacked and his army beaten in Port-au-Prince. The United States took up the cause of General Nord Alexis and imposed a naval embargo on Firmin's troops in his last two strongholds. In exchange for this hand, Washington received guarantees on interests in the area.

Berlin also sided with General Nord Alexis and launched a warship to attack Admiral Killick,[121] Anténor Firmin's ally. A few hours before, the admiral had confiscated a German ship transporting weapons for the interim government. Tracked down and cornered, rather than surrendering, Killick chose to blow up his ship with himself and the spoils on board. This was the turning point for this power struggle. Anténor Firmin lost his strike force, threw in the towel, and left for exile on Saint-Thomas Island. His supporters, who remained in his Le Cap bastion, were persecuted. The city was in turmoil, following a series of denunciations and trials. Weapons were even found in the possession of a pharmacist.

This was heartbreaking for Joseph, who no longer recognized the Le Cap that he'd left barely a year ago. He was afraid for his mother, although she was not politically active: Euzélie's name was Laroche, and she had family ties with Cincinnatus Leconte. Joseph feared attacks from fanatics or revanchists. But what could he do? He asked himself over and over. He was thousands of kilometers away from home and couldn't in any way influence the course of events. What was one to do when adults were seized by folly? What was one to do, other than duly note that General Nord Alexis was the new president? Hope, pray, and focus on school.

Compared to the terrible news that arrived bit by bit from Haiti, the scandal that hit the school in Beauvais seemed less important to him.

On August 11, 1902, at 6:00 p.m., the public prosecutor, a committing magistrate and a court clerk showed up at Institution du Saint-Esprit, following a complaint made by a "five- or six-year-old" girl who alleged that a servant at the school had behaved inappropriately toward her. "They had to gather the servants," Father Heitz, the school superior, recounted. "The little girl pointed to one of them and said having witnessed the poor devil make naughty gestures from a window on the second floor. After two hours of questioning, the servant was put at the disposal of justice for ten days. This is how we prevented the trouble of a broad daylight arrest."

In the end, not one, but two servants, of Belgian and Luxembourgian origins, respectively, were summoned. The news caused a sensation. The next day, the whole of Beauvais talked of nothing else. Some maintained that the child was sexually assaulted by "three Spiritan brothers." Others insisted that the culprits had run away. With the school's reputation at stake, Father Heitz was upset: "That day sent me into a terrible panic," he wrote. "From the morning the most ludicrous rumors had been circulating in town about the public prosecutor's visit. They were saying that three little girls had been assaulted in the brothers' house and tearful friends were coming for news." And, as if this was not enough, the media took hold of what it already considered a "scandal." On August 12, the local newspaper *La République de l'Oise* made this "mysterious affair" its headline. The next day, the national daily paper *L'Intransigeant*[122] in turn put on its front page this "serious moral affair."

• • •

It was not the first time the media reported the legal troubles of the Institution du Saint-Esprit. Ten years earlier, *La République de l'Oise* had relayed an incident that had occurred during a walk in November 1891, when some sixth graders had thrown gravel from a bridge to a railway below, while a locomotive was passing by. The train driver had been slightly hurt. He had then made a complaint against the children and the priest who was chaperoning the trip. Of course, *La République de l'Oise* had swiftly reported on the father of Saint-Esprit being in criminal court. The court had subsequently declared the priest liable and sentenced the parents of the students to pay damages.

But things went differently in the case of the little girl. After a few weeks of the unexpected report, the case deflated all by itself. The court discovered "that all this noise had no foundation, and that the testimonies were shaky." The child's mother, a prostitute, finally admitted in front of that court that the little girl was "a vicious liar." It was, in fact, a "frame-up" aimed at turning public opinion against the Spiritans and "chase them away" from the town, after having "dragged their name through mud." The case was thus closed.

What to think of all this? Joseph Laroche who, like his French schoolmates, had witnessed the events, was alarmed. Why so much hate? How can one deploy so much energy just to hurt others? He did not understand.

In the stories from his childhood, the animals at least could make a distinction between wrong and malice. Was it possible that we might be lower than them?

By the end of summer break, however, the scandal involving the little girl was already forgotten. At Institution du Saint-Esprit, classes resumed on Wednesday, October 1, 1902.

Three days later, Father Heitz was happy: "Our new school year is better than expected: 116 students now, and they will be 120 very soon," he wrote. Unfortunately, on November 7, Heitz was disillusioned when he discovered that the reputation of the school was once again threatened, this time from the inside. As it turned out, the "elders" in the school had been behaving inappropriately since the beginning of the year, revealing its dark side. "The principal helped us discover a secret association—with statutes and a president, whose only goal is to corrupt the younger students," an outraged superior reported to the Parisian management. "They did not succeed, but we have expelled the three troublemakers of this secret club."

Although Joseph Laroche was an "elder" like the "three troublemakers," he kept a distance from the schoolmates whose status as "elders" sometimes provoked vanity or even maliciousness, and sometimes yielded to the temptation of humiliating the new students. For Joseph, only one thing mattered: maintain a personal code of conduct in order to get his *baccalaur*éat and soon enter an engineering school. He must do as well as, if not better than, the past year. Between sleeping and eating, and learning, his days were completely full anyway. Throughout the year and in addition to the classes, the Institution du Saint-Esprit offered to the "elders" a series of conferences on comprehensive themes, such as: The Paris youngster. The parallel between Michelet and Fustel de Coulanges. Intelligence and French adolescence. The Second Empire's Court.

Saint Vincent de Paul, by unknown artist. Published in *Magasin Pittoresque*,
Paris, 1840.

Saint Vincent de Paul.

Portrait and autograph by French poet Edmond Eugène Alexis Rostand.
Illustration from *Niva* magazine, publishing house A.F. Marx, St. Petersburg,
Russia, 1913.

On Fridays, the "elders" also tended to the poor during visits with the brothers of Saint-Vincent de Paul. Those brothers had been active in Beauvais since 1629, when their founder Vincent de Paul himself came to establish "charity brotherhoods" in the parishes at the request of the bishop, who was dealing with generalized begging. Institution du Saint-Esprit considered the weekly participation of its students in this unique program a way to "maintain their piety." The school believed that charity began with the poor.

The picture of a young Haitian sent every week to the bedside of destitute Frenchmen could seem paradoxical today considering the situation in Port-au-Prince in the 2010s. But, at the time, Joseph Laroche's presence did not surprise anyone. He was not different from the others: he was a "rich kid." As for Joseph, seeing these poor people was in sharp contrast with the beautiful idea he had of France—the rich and prosperous nation portrayed by his uncle, Nemours Auguste, and all those who'd come back from Paris. That poor people could exist in this country as well was a true revelation for the young Haitian.

The real paradox, in fact, lay somewhere else. The dedication of the students to the poor was not only meant to maintain their piety; it also allowed them to take part in the work of the brothers of Saint-Vincent de Paul, whose goal was the "evangelization of the working-class people."

In other words, every Friday, when Joseph Laroche visited with his schoolmates the indigents of Beauvais, he really was putting himself in a missionary's shoes.

This role reversal escaped him at the time, but it was a little as if the word "black" had been replaced by "white" and the words "Africa" and "colonies" by "Europe" and "France" in the Congregation of Saint-Esprit rule enacted by Father Libermann in 1851: "Evangelize the poor, that is our general goal. However, missions are our main objective, and in our missions we have chosen the most miserable and most abandoned souls. The Divine Providence has given us work with the blacks, either from

Africa or the Colonies. They are, without dispute, the most miserable and the most abandoned, until today."

In addition to those visits, the school "elders" also organized shows for the benefit of the destitute. For example, they performed on stage excerpts from *L'aiglon*,[123] Edmond Rostand's drama, or *Les Erinnyes*, Leconte de Lisle's ancient tragedy in verse. The shows were performed for the parents and the other students of the school, who also contributed to the cause: the sophomores paid two francs and the juniors three francs.

■ ■ ■

For Joseph Laroche, each day spent at Institution du Saint-Esprit was an enriching one, except for the time in French class when he read a text titled "Napoleon the First, Writer and Orator" that praised "the picturesque, sober, and true style" of *Bonaparte's Memoirs* in which he recounted his greatest military campaigns. The title cast a shadow on Joseph's spirits. He had not forgotten that this same Napoleon had had his hero Toussaint Louverture deported. The very name of the Frenchman angered him. However, every time Joseph thought of him, he comforted himself with the idea that Jean-Jacques Dessalines, the "Father of Haitian Independence," had given the French emperor a taste of his own medicine.

■ ■ ■

As the new school year started in 1902, the French were plunged into a vast school reform. The government sought to modernize secondary education to better cater to the real needs of the country and adapt to the present-day world. It wanted to prepare the students, not only for liberal careers or teaching professions, as it had done so far, but also "for the economic life and for action." With that purpose, a commission headed by a parliamentarian had been put into place by Georges Leygues, the Minister of Public Education. The group had heard from nearly two hundred individuals, among them politicians, academicians, university professors and secondary-school teachers, principals, congregation members, and representatives from the agricultural and commercial spheres.

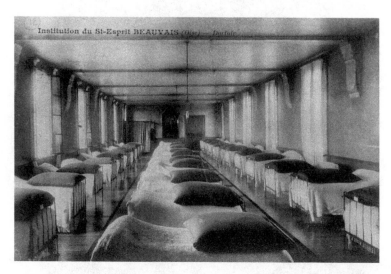

Dormitories at the Institution du Saint-Esprit.

For Joseph Laroche, each day spent at Institution du Saint-Esprit was an enriching one, except for the time in French class when he read a text titled "Napoleon the First, Writer and Orator" that praised "the picturesque, sober, and true style" of *Bonaparte's Memoirs* in which he recounted his greatest military campaigns.

Napoleon Bonaparte.

"Joseph Laroche had not forgotten that this same Napoleon had had his hero Toussaint Louverture deported. The very name of the Frenchman angered him. However, every time Joseph thought of him, he comforted himself with the idea that Jean-Jacques Dessalines, the 'Father of Haitian Independence,' had given the French emperor a taste of his own medicine."

Between old and new schools of thought, positions were sometimes divided, and the arguments engaged in publicly. The old-school advocates defended the preeminence of Latin[124] over French and refused to allow the system to change, fearing that the change would lead to decadence; the country, they believed, would not recover from turning its back on ancient ethics, superior to all others. The new-school champions, on the other hand, recommended a new balance that favored the French language; they wanted French to acquire the same legitimacy as Latin, a dead language no longer used by the elites and aristocrats—a vestige of an outmoded past. According to them, living languages such as English or German were to be allowed more room, and the same went for science.

The debate lasted several months, until a compromise was found and the reform promulgated in a decree. Two cycles now existed: the first one included a section without Latin among the existing two sections, while the second cycle was divided in four sections, one without Latin.

■ ■ ■

At Institution du Saint-Esprit, the students received a daily portion of bread at the refectory, in the morning, at noon, and in the evening, because it was deemed good for balance and rich in vitamins. Joseph and the others also enjoyed games on Thursdays and Sundays, when they met on the large lawn at the Saint-Lucien abbey. *Panem et circenses.* Bread and games. This was one of the many Latin expressions Joseph Laroche knew well. He'd heard it for the first time in Haiti, when the teacher had jeered at the way Roman emperors chose the easiest way to amuse the people and attract favors in return: they distributed "bread" and organized "games." In any case, at the school in Beauvais, moments of leisure were important to the Spiritans because they cleared the mind and rested the body. *Mens sana in corpore sano.* A healthy mind in a healthy body.

That year, the students practiced a new game, called the shield, inspired by the chivalrous spirit of the Middle Ages. The students formed two camps, the blue and the red, and held wooden shields to protect themselves from sock balls, weighted with sand, that opponents threw at each other. The teams were separated by an imaginary sea, represented by two ropes three meters apart. Above the "sea" were two wooden bridges on the grass, marking the border between the two countries. This was where practically everything happened: the student-soldiers fought on these narrow bridges, without mercy, shield against shield. The goal was to enter enemy territory, capture two adversary flags, and bring them back to one's own camp without being hit three times. Every time a student was hit, he lost a "parcel of freedom" and took off one of the three pieces of cloth affixed to his shoulder. After the third time, he ended up in prison.

A priest oversaw the smooth running of this rough game, which aimed at conveying the virtues of suffering, resilience, and courage. Joseph Laroche loved it tremendously. At each victory of their camp, Joseph's teammates happily yelled the name of Bayard, "the fearless knight beyond reproach." But Joseph was instead thinking of King Christophe at these moments. To say that hardly fifty years before, he thought, one could be dubbed prince, count, or duke, by a sovereign.

During the 1902 school year, the French united around the school reform but were still divided about the Associations Act.

In June, by decree, the new Council President Émile Combes had closed 135 religious schools. Since then, he had published a circular ordering the closure of 2,500 more schools.

In Quimper, a hundred independent schools closed their doors. From one day to another, six hundred nuns and twenty thousand students were left high and dry. In Nîmes, four hundred nuns and seven thousand students were put out on the streets after the closure of eighty schools. It was a hard blow for the episcopacy, who accused Combes of "persecution." It was a social and human tragedy.

In Beauvais, Institution du Saint-Esprit had yet to close, but a worrisome "sectarian climate" could be felt. "During the school years 1901 and 1902, one could feel the terrors of the moment. None of the families was any longer free to entrust us with their children," Father Le Floch, a former superior of the school, explained. But many of the parents did not give in to fear. "My husband gave up a promotion rather than agreeing to send our children to public school," a mother confided at the beginning of the school year in 1902. "We will not have a big fortune to leave them, but at least they will have been raised in a Christian manner. I hope that later they will bless us."

· · ·

The closing of so many schools in France was unnerving. Although Joseph Laroche feared the worst, it was out of the question to give in to panic: he wanted to remain focused on his goal while waiting for the public to review the case of Institution du Saint-Esprit. It would take a few months, the administration told him. In the meantime, the uncertainties that weighed on his future motivated him, rather than discouraged him. He gave himself over to readings and mathematical formulas, deepening his knowledge of French regions, and he aced all topics during the school year.

Joseph remained buried in his books and notebooks until a surprising incident distracted him from his learning: out of nowhere, his father wrote. He sent Joseph a telegram to announce the birth of his second half-brother Carlet, born on June 14, 1903, in Le Cap. If Joseph gladly welcomed the news, he was, on the other hand, surprised by the note. For the first time, his father seemed to think of him as a member of the family. In fact, Raoul Auguste did not stop with that one telegram. Moved by a newfound enthusiasm, he sent a second announcement to the Beauvais boarder—one that left the young man speechless. After seventeen long years, he shared with Joseph his intention to finally acknowledge him and give him his name.

Joseph was shocked by the surprising turnaround. For so long, he had desperately waited for a gesture from his father. It had never come—until now. But, for the teenager Joseph had become, this announcement came too late. He realized that the bond he had formed with his mother was enough, and he meant for his life to remain the way it was.

"I carry the name of my mother," Joseph replied mischievously, "and this name, Laroche, is more august in Cap-Haïtien than the name Auguste."

In other words, he preferred to keep Euzélie's surname: not only was he proud of his mother's accomplishments and the connections her family had, "Laroche" was the umbilical cord that linked him in an unfailing love for the person who gave him life.

. . .

After the adoption of the Associations Act, after the closing of the congregational schools everywhere in France, after long uncertainty as to the future of the Beauvais school, the Spiritans finally learned where they stood. On November 4, 1903, the superior general received the following letter from the government: "On October 1, 1901, you applied for the authorization provided for in Article thirteen paragraph two of the Act of July 1, 1901, for twelve schools that are part of your Congregation," the Council President, Minister of the Interior and for Religious Affairs, Émile Combes,[125] wrote. "After review of the paperwork produced in support of this application and the results of the examination that was performed, I have decided that there was no need to transfer the files to the state council for the solicited authorizations. Consequently, I have the honor to notify you that your application is rejected." Émile Combes also reminded the superior general that "any individual who, without the required authorization, opens or administers a congregational school, regardless of its nature" is subject to severe punishment: "a penalty from sixteen to five thousand francs and imprisonment from six days to a year."

In other words, the letter from Combes ordered the teachers of Institution du Saint-Esprit, mostly priests, to leave the premises. Two days later, without allowing enough time for the superior general of the Spiritans in Paris to inform the Beauvais school management, public law enforcement relayed the message. Father Le Floch recounted the evening of November 6, when the police captain came to notify Father Malleret, the superior, of the Ministry's refusal to submit to the State council the school's authorization application. "We were also the first to receive in that occasion the official notice of closing of eleven other house of the Congregation," he wrote. "The certainty and extent of this misfortune plunged us in a deep sadness."

■ ■ ■

In Beauvais, the news of the school closure came as a bombshell. The teachers and parents were disconcerted, and the students distraught. What would become of the pupils? How would they finish the school year? Even Joseph Laroche, who until then had kept his distance from the fights between the political powers and the French clergy, took part in the debate. He'd come to France with a specific goal: to get an engineering diploma. His mother had spent a lot for that. He himself had made big sacrifices, cramming relentlessly with few vacations. Now a senior, he was to take the *baccalauréat*[126] in a few months.

He would not accept having his future ruined. Besides, none of this made sense to Joseph: how could France afford to interfere with the education of thousands of its children, while the Haitian government sacrificed a fortune to educate at least a few hundred, dedicating a major part of the national budget to the support of missionaries in the country?

Privilege, Joseph thought. Not everyone had it. As a Haitian, he certainly didn't. Now he understood why so many of his uncles entertained the fantasy of, one day, getting into politics at the highest level.

■ ■ ■

Map of Beauvais

Topographical Map of Oise, in France. From *Dictionary of Words and Things* published by
Larive and Fleury in 1895

Beauvais's Provincial museum in Oise, Picardy, France.

The decision was brutal, and Joseph Laroche didn't think it could be appealed. He reminisced about his childhood, about the folktales and the fables he still loved and the lessons they taught. *La raison du plus fort est toujours la meilleure.* Was it true, then, that "might is right," that the powerful—in this case, the public power embodied by the government—could do what they wished, unchallenged? Could they really refuse Spiritan fathers the right to continue educating children and thus sentence Institution du Saint-Esprit to closing its doors?

In the end, however, Institution du Saint-Esprit, proved the shrewder. The Spiritans had been expecting the minister's rejection. At the start of the new school year of 1903, they had already recruited a new staff of lay people and secular priests, which allowed the school to remain open, because it was—technically—no longer run by Spiritans. As for the closing of the other twelve Spiritan schools following the Act of 1901, many saw it as a relative blessing. For many years, the schools belonging to the Congregation had been in deep in debt and chronic deficit. As explained by historian Paul Airiau, "expenses decreased, with liquidations being done in acceptable conditions. It also solved, once and for all, the opposition between missionaries and teachers."

• • •

On December 30, 1903, the day before the Spiritans' departure, a sober farewell ceremony was held at the Beauvais school. For Joseph Laroche and for the "elders" of the school, the departure of these Spiritans, who had led them, supported them, advised them, listened to them, as well as punished them, for two and a half years, was heartbreaking. Father Malleret introduced to the students his successor, Abbot Leclerc, and the short speeches each of them gave caused many tears. The students knew that nothing would be as before; they might as well get this last semester and the *baccalaur*éat, over with as quickly as possible.

Joseph Laroche felt even more motivated in this home stretch. He passed his "bac" exam without any difficulty and attended the prize-giving ceremony. That evening, the Haitian graduate caught himself singing with

more spirit than ever the school anthem, with the amazing lyrics that he
had learned shortly after his arrival in Beauvais in 1901:

Soon, away from these tranquil shores
Scattered at the discretion of the storms
In the middle of raging waters
Remember the Holy Spirit

From the heavens, in the dark night
He will come down, dispersing darkness
Giving us back hope and peace
s in the happy days of Beauvais

VI. There Is Wind and Joy

For the school year of 1904, Joseph Laroche stayed in Beauvais. He attended the Institut Agricole de Beauvais, run by the Brothers of Christian Schools, to begin training in agronomic engineering. The school, three hundred meters from the train station, welcomed only boarders, the majority the "sons of well-to-do families or owners who wanted to learn how to manage a rural estate." Admission was competitive. After the "bac," Joseph had spent his vacation preparing for the exam, which included French and scientific compositions.

Only applicants mastering the principles of inorganic chemistry, the metric system, practical geometry, algebra, physics, and natural science were admitted at Institut Agricole de Beauvais.

Training lasted three years, with a theoretical component taught on-site and a practical component provided on five neighboring farms. Soon, Joseph Laroche would know everything about arboriculture, land survey, botany, geology, horticulture, and entomology. In addition to those new subjects, he would study applied mathematics, linear drawing, architecture, agricultural law, and social economics. Independently of these classes, all the students were required to enroll for a religious education class, as mandated by the school regulations. In short, for Joseph Laroche, other than the radically different curriculum, nothing had changed: the Institute maintained the spirit of the secondary school years.

The Laroche family lived in Villejuif, a commune in the southern suburbs of Paris, France, about a dozen kilometers from the Saint-Lazare train station. Villejuif means "Jewtown," but there is no record of medieval Jews having lived in Villejuif. Jewish-language columnist Philologos questions the origins of the name: "And what about the fact that, *ville* being grammatically feminine, 'Jewtown' should have been *Villejuive* and not *Villejuif*? Was the 'v' devoiced into an 'f' over time? Was the original name *ville des juifs* or *ville aux juifs*, 'the town of the Jews,' from which the *des* (of) or *aux* (pertaining or belonging to) was eventually dropped?"

JOSEPH LAROCHE, BY LOCATION

CAP-HAÏTIEN

Founded in 1670 by the French, and located in the mountainous Northern region of Haiti, Cap-Haïtien was originally known as Cap-Français and gained early renown as the "Paris of the Antilles," for its stunning architecture and cultural offerings. It served as capital of Saint-Domingue until 1770 and was the scene of slave uprisings in 1791. The city was razed by French and Haitian troops in 1802 but was later rebuilt under the reign of King Henri Christophe. After the revolution (around 1820), he proclaimed it the capital of the Northern Kingdom of Haiti. Cap-Haïtien was Haiti's most important city for a long time until Port-au-Prince relegated it to second place. Joseph Laroche was born in Cap-Haïtien, which is often referred as Le Cap or Okap.

BEAUVAIS

Beauvais is a city and commune in northern France. Joseph Laroche attended the Institut Agricole de Beauvais to begin training as an agronomic engineer. One of the city's landmarks, the Beauvais Cathedral, which has been described as "ambitious and gravity-defying," boasts the record for the highest ceiling in a gothic choir. In fact, it was the tallest monument in the Christendom for four consecutive years until its lantern tower tragically collapsed.

LILLE

Joseph Laroche attended Faculté Catholique des Hautes Études Industrielles in Lille, 150 kilometers from Beauvais. Lille is a true college town—over 100,000 of its inhabitants are students. Lille is renowned for its summer markets, festivals and concerts. One of its most notable events is the Braderie de Lille, the largest flea market in all of Europe, which takes place at the end of every summer. Café de Bellevue on the Grand Place, and Café Jean near the theater were Joseph Laroche's favorite hangout places in Lille.

VILLEJUIF

The Laroche family lived in Villejuif, a commune in the southern suburbs of Paris, France, about a dozen kilometers from the Saint Lazare train station. Villejuif means "Jewtown," but there is no record of medieval Jews having lived in Villejuif. Jewish-language columnist Philologos questions the origins of the name: "And what about the fact that, ville being grammatically feminine, 'Jewtown' should have been Villejuive and not Villejuif? Was the 'v' devoiced into an 'f' over time? Was the original name ville des juifs or ville aux juifs, 'the town of the Jews,' from which the des (of) or aux (pertaining or belonging to) was eventually dropped?"

However, change came two years later, during an outing to a Parisian suburb, where Joseph was taking English classes. He befriended a young man, Maurice Lafargue, who invited him to the home of his father, André Lafargue, a wine trader. The appointment was in Villejuif, at 131 Grande Rue, now Avenue Jean-Jaurès, for a very pleasant lunch. Joseph Laroche was on cloud nine. Not only did he enjoy the excellent meal, which was a change from the insipid refectory menu, but he really liked Juliette, the strikingly beautiful person who had prepared it. She was André Lafargue's daughter and had been the light of his life since the death of his wife.

Between Joseph and Juliette, it was love at first sight. Did Maurice Lafargue notice the attraction between his sister and his friend? Most likely. He knew her too well. Did André Lafargue understand that the two young people were attracted to each other? Maybe. Although a widower, he still remembered the tremors of love. After only exchanging a few words, Joseph and Juliette couldn't stop smiling at each other. When the meal ended, it was to their great disappointment. To the young man going back to Beauvais, Juliette promised to write. He promised to reply. But for now, he had to concentrate on the thesis he was soon to defend. If he passed, convincing the jury of the quality of his work, his diploma was guaranteed.

Thanks to maturity and experience, on "D-day," Joseph Laroche obtained a perfect score. He did not shake. He did not falter, as he'd thoroughly mastered his subject. When Joseph Laroche called his mother on that day to share the good news, she cried. So many sacrifices for such wonderful results! She was proud of her son. Little Joseph, whom she used to pamper not long ago in Le Cap, was now a big man somewhere in Beauvais. He was an engineer—unbelievable! And Joseph Laroche did not want to stop there. He meant to expand his training by taking classes as an unregistered student at Faculté Catholique des Hautes Etudes Industrielles in Lille, 150 kilometers from the small rural town of Beauvais. In September of 1907, the young agronomist reached his new destination and settled into a boarding house for students. Joseph Laroche found himself in a different, mesmerizing world. Everything in the northern metropolis was bigger, taller, larger, and there were ten times as many inhabitants. They swarmed everywhere.

In Lille,[127] the spirit was also different. Education was modern, dynamic, and even avant-garde, not only in the university sphere that he was entering, but also in the other schools in the area.

In the neighboring locality of Laon, for example, the school principal authorized the students to play football on the playground because he preferred "the inconvenience of a broken window to the widespread melancholy." The teachers did not hesitate to complement their classes with philosophical discussions with students in a street or under a tree at the public garden. One of them, soon-to-be writer Jules Romains, brought his sociology classes to life by taking his student on bank and factory tours. "If such initiatives that seemed to us surprisingly ahead of their time could be undertaken, it was because they were approved and even encouraged by three superintendents: Henri Couat (1887–1890), Charles Bayet (1891–1896) and Georges Lyon (1903–1924)," archivist René Robinet noted.

In Lille, innovation was constant. From the start, the city adapted as much as possible to the great changes brought forth by the first two industrial revolutions, marked by the invention of the steam engine and the first appearance of electricity, which had become the driving force. These two technological developments benefited the local economy, which was booming. Factories were sprouting like mushrooms. "In 1840, nearly all the factories in the area were equipped with steam engines. In Lille, from 1848 to 1866, their number increased from 130 to 576 for a number of factories that increased from 129 to 343," academic Marie-Thérèse Pourprix explained. And to safely maintain and run these complex machines, specialists and skilled workers were needed.

This prompted the opening in 1854 of École des Arts Industriels et des Mines and of the School of Science, where chemist and physicist Louis Pasteur[128] was the first dean.

In 1858, a school for drivers and mechanics opened, teaching the operation of steam engines.

Street in a Lille neighborhood in France, with typical small brick houses where workers used to live during the industrial revolution. Joseph Laroche attended Faculté Catholique des Hautes Études Industrielles in Lille, 150 kilometers from Beauvais. Lille is a true college town—over 100,000 of its inhabitants are students. The town is renowned for its summer markets, festivals and concerts. One of its most notable events is the Braderie de Lille, the largest flea market in all of Europe, which takes place at the end of every summer. Café de Bellevue on the Grand Place, and Café Jean near the theater were Joseph Laroche's favorite hangout places in Lille.

Lyderic, a legendary figure tied to the foundation of Lille. Created by Best and Leloir, published in *Magasin Pittoresque*, Paris, 1840.

Old illustration of charity food distribution in Lille, France. Published in
L'Illustration: Journal Universel, Paris, 1968.

In 1885, Joseph entered the brand-new engineering school, which aimed to adapt to the needs of manufacturers and owners, with courses ranging from fluid mechanics to energy to public works. Of course, everything was different here for Joseph, although certain landmarks did remind him of his home country, helping him with his transition. First, the classes took place close to a military structure dating from the seventeenth century. Everyone called it the "Citadel," a word that reminded him of Le Cap and King Christophe. In Lille, he also renewed his passion for cockfighting. Although the brutal blood sport had been forbidden in the area since 1852, people hurried on Sundays to see the gallinaceous birds fight in the back rooms of cabarets, until the big yearly contests that took place at the Lille racetrack. The greatest cockfighters from the north of France and from Belgium presented their animals to fight on that day in public.

The "Three Happy Days,"[129] Lille Carnival, also immersed Joseph in Haitian-like exuberance! The crowds dressed up to dance and parade in the streets at the rhythm of the floats. In the neighboring city of Dunkerque, pranksters were on the lookout for anyone without an umbrella as they started the traditional throwing of herring at the end of the show.

Joseph Laroche's year in Lille was enriching. While educating himself, he discovered a new way of life, free from the constraints imposed in Beauvais. He now slept in a room by himself. He was free to wake up and go to bed at a time of his choosing, free to attend or miss classes, free to come and go as he pleased. He discovered the bistros, where one could read the newspaper in peace or drink with friends. He navigated between Café de Bellevue, located on the Grand-Place, and Café Jean, near the theater. After class, he sometimes cloistered himself in L'Impérial, the famous movie theater, to watch the latest comedy or drama.

Portrait of Louis Pasteur.

Louis Pasteur was a French chemist and microbiologist who made many important discoveries related to the immune system, vaccinations, chemistry and the nature of diseases. In 1848 he became professor of chemistry at the University of Strasbourg and in 1854 he became dean of the faculty of sciences at Lille University. A quote from Louis Pasteur: "I am utterly convinced that Science and Peace will triumph over Ignorance and War, that nations will eventually unite not to destroy but to edify, and that the future will belong to those who have done the most for the sake of suffering humanity."

He was also in love. Not a day had gone by without Joseph thinking of Juliette. She wrote him emotional letters, which he answered with passion. She swore only by him, and he by her. Sometimes, on weekends, he went to see her in Villejuif, where they spent long, happy moments together, well aware, however, of the ways this intensifying idyll seriously interfered with Joseph Laroche's plans. To him, it was obvious that after his studies in France, he would go back to work in Le Cap. Beauvais and Lille both constituted a hiatus, as he couldn't imagine a life anywhere but in Haiti. If he married Juliette, as he also contemplated, would she agree to follow him to the Caribbean? Not only did she fear such a great change, she also worried about her aging father, André Lafargue. Who would watch over him? Her brother Maurice could take care of him, sure. But, regardless of his good intentions, Juliette didn't believe him capable of the same attention she'd demonstrated toward her father.

In the end, news from Haiti forced Joseph to make a decision. On January 8, 1908, President Nord Alexis was overthrown by putschist Antoine Simon.[130] He was forced to exile, just like his Minister of Interior, who was no other than Cincinnatus Leconte, the husband of Joséphine Laroche, Joseph's dear cousin. This situation did not encourage Joseph Laroche to return to Le Cap, especially as he was preoccupied by some of the logistics: how could he get a good position upon his return if they assumed his loyalty to Leconte, even though Joseph was not involved in politics? Wasn't it better to wait for the fire to be put out, before going back to Haiti? He worried, as did many others in the throes of the same anguish.

His uncle, Dr. Jean-Baptiste Déjoie Laroche, for instance, still lived in exile in Paris, where he'd withdrawn after a streak of bad luck with a previous Haitian president a few years before. He, too, was waiting for the tide to turn, so that he could go back to Le Cap. President Tirésias Simon Sam had also taken refuge in Paris after the shooting that had broken out in the Parliament when he'd announced his resignation in May 1902. His fallen successor, Pierre Nord Alexis, chose a completely different sanctuary: he settled with Cincinnatus Leconte in Kingston, Jamaica.[131] In fact, Jamaica, located 160 kilometers from Haiti, was at the time the preferred destination of deposed Haitian heads of state. As explained by former minister Jean Victor Généus,[132] from 1888 to 1913, among the eight presidents who succeeded each other in power in Haiti, five were forced to seek refuge in Jamaica,

Of course, this political instability was due in part to Haitian rivalries, but it was also encouraged—and even provoked—by the big powers. Généus denounced constant American interference, pointing out that the country's financial institutions were controlled by the Europeans, who used all sorts of maneuvers to reinforce their position and ensure juicy profits.

But in Kingston, where they took up residence, the Haitian exiles only thought of one thing: recruit mercenaries to take over Haiti and get their power back. There, it was not rare for a fallen president, upon disembarking in Jamaica, to cross paths with his successor embarking for Port-au-Prince, a mob of soldiers in tow.

The *New York Times* reported that those returning to Haiti occupied the upper deck on the boat. They had well-cut mustaches "à la française." Crew members brought them champagne and rum.

"In the opposite direction, the disembarking exiles created a pathetic scene: they arrived to Kingston with arms in slings, their heads bandaged, and their clothes in shreds. They deserved no sympathy because they were going to spend their time in Jamaica without working—waiting for their turn."

■ ■ ■

On March 18, 1908, Joseph Laroche married Juliette Lafargue at the Villejuif church. He was twenty-two years old and she nineteen. The ceremony was simple, just like the bride and groom. Joseph's mother could not be in attendance, but she sent her well wishes to the couple, expressing her impatience to see them soon in Le Cap. As for Joseph's father-in-law, he was emotional: he'd married off his only daughter, which was not a small thing. The reception, the dinner, the ball...everything went perfectly.

View of Kingston in Jamaica. From *Magasin Pittoresque*, 1836.

Jamaica is an island country situated in the Caribbean Sea. It is the third-largest island of the
Greater Antilles and the fourth-largest island country in the Caribbean. Jamaica lies about 191
kilometers west of Hispaniola. Nord Alexis and Cincinnatus Leconte sought refuge in Jamaica
after losing power in Haiti.

The newlyweds were beaming, and the guests rejoiced. Joseph even demonstrated a few steps of the merengue, a Haitian dance, leading Juliette on the floor, the party going on well into the night. Then Joseph and Juliette headed home, not too far from the wedding venue, at 131 Grande Rue in Villejuif. André Lafargue was very happy to house them, inviting them to stay for as long as they wanted, even after Joseph was able to support his family.

For Joseph, once again, it was the beginning of a new life. In the following days, he started looking for a job, sending application letters everywhere.

These letters always started with, "I have the honor to seek" and often ended with, "Please find enclosed a stamp for the reply."

Because Joseph was not French and had no professional experience to cast a favorable light on him, he most likely included a letter of recommendation from his father-in-law, which seems to have been the custom for foreigners married into French families. An Algerian, who applied for the same company, Les Entreprises Nord-Sud, attached a letter from his father-in-law, a French grain seller, who wrote: "I have the honor to introduce you to an individual of good character, good morality, and good reputation. He started as my assistant; as he gained my trust, through his hard work, his zeal, and his honesty, I later entrusted him with a store that he managed alone, without the need for oversight. I can only praise his behavior."

Joseph Laroche's application was accepted by Nord-Sud, one of the companies that held contracts for the "underground electric railway," today's Parisian subway. At the time, the construction of lines and operation of the network were left to private companies, and Nord-Sud had been awarded three projects: line A, from Porte de la Chapelle to Porte de Versailles, via Montmartre and Montparnasse; line B, connecting Saint-Lazare to Porte de Clichy via Porte de Saint-Ouen; and line C, from Montparnasse to Porte de Vanves. Joseph Laroche was be assigned to the design of line A, along with several other engineers—a complicated task, because the subsoil at the site was chalky in some places, so the line couldn't run straight.

In addition, between the Chambres des Députés and Concorde stations, they were to dig under the Seine. On some evenings, Joseph came home with the line's blueprints to research the best solutions late into the night. He compared notes the next day with other team members. "In the 90s, I went to the Laroche residence in Villejuif, and I saw those blueprints that Joseph had drawn and that his family had kept," legal practitioner Christina Schutt recounts.

Joseph Laroche's contract with Nord-Sud was short-term, but the experience left its mark. He rubbed shoulders with the working class of France, those individuals who were exploited and thrown away at the first mistake: laborers, stonemasons, roadworkers who exhausted themselves, digging kilometers of tunnels in inhumane conditions. Many of them died, electrocuted or cut in half by an engine.

Nobody really cared, although *L'Illustration*[133] did make mention—once—of the fate of these thousands of nameless people who toiled under the earth. The newspaper sent two correspondents into the gloomy tunnels to report on the courage of the workers. Despite the purposely poetic style of the reporter, the article sent shivers down the spine: "Both the mythological den that forged the cyclops and the mysterious caves of the Nibelung are nothing in comparison to these tunnels that descend to eight meters under the Seine. Only a long chimney brings oxygen into the work chamber, where powerful machines are compressing the air, which becomes too heavy for the lungs. When one enters this metal tunnel, the pressure becomes uncomfortable and brings the strangest of feelings. In the light of electric lamps, about thirty laborers are at work. They hold picks and hammers, creating with their rhythmic blows a deafening noise, as they progressively dig into the ground."

. . .

Napoleon III train. Created by Gaildrau, published in
L'Illustration: Journal Universel, Paris, 1858

Diner-coach, terrace-coach and lounge-coach in imperial train offered from
railways company to Napoleon III. Created by Godefroy-Durand, published in
L'Illustration: Journal Universel, Paris, 1857.

Building railway bridge in Faubourg Saint-Antoine, Paris. Created by Parent,
published in *L'Illustration: Journal Universel*, Paris, 1858.

Train transit on railway iron bridge over the Garonne in Bordeaux, France.
Created by Gaildrau, published in *L'Illustration: Journal Universel*,
Paris, 1860.

On October 20, 1908, upon returning home, Joseph Laroche learned in a telegram from his mother that Raoul Auguste had passed away. Although the man was more of a stranger than a father, Joseph was shaken. He was particularly sad for the four children of the man he never knew. He thought about Carlet, the youngest; he wished he could comfort him and his sisters, like a big brother should. For Joseph, this was the start of a season of grief, as Lisettine passed away soon after—a hard blow. His grandmother represented his childhood: she'd fed his memory, his imagination, his life. He wished he was in Le Cap to see her once more, laugh at the good memories, and cry as he accompanied her to her final home. But, that was not possible, and he felt miserable.

However, Joseph's distress eventually gave way to happiness: his daughter Simone was born on February 19, 1909. Such emotion! He'd never experienced such joy in his life. He, usually so calm and poised, could barely keep his composure around the midwife. At the time, most births occurred at home. With early-enough notice, a midwife was sent to the bedside of the woman in labor to facilitate the delivery. In an emergency situation, however, the family was to manage on its own until the arrival of a medical team. Thankfully, Simone arrived without any incident, and her birth brought sunny days in the life of Joseph Laroche, who had felt a little depressed in this beginning of 1909. Since the end of his contract with Nord-Sud, his employment had been desperately sporadic. He had a hard time finding a job, and when he did find one, he was ill-treated by his employers.

In the only interview she gave in 1995, in which she briefly mentioned the subject, Louise Laroche explained that her father faced "racial prejudice" at that time. "Joseph would find small jobs, but his employers always claimed that he was young and inexperienced, so they could pay him low wages."

In 1909 racial prejudice was, unfortunately, very common in France. The press and the colonial literature reported that blacks belonged to an "indisputably inferior race." French and European scientists even claimed that they were not men but "apes," which was the reason why they were found in "human zoos." Indeed, during those years, Parisian families rushed on Sundays to the Jardin d'Acclimatation near the Bois de Boulogne to discover with excitement Nubians, Congolese, Somalis, Zulus, or Hottentots who were exhibited in cages like "wild animals." The discovery of this reality, and more generally of racism, was hard on Joseph Laroche, who was plunged into a whole new world he'd been ill prepared for. At the school in Beauvais, he had never felt like a reject or a foreigner. In that protected place, that Catholic cocoon that was the boarding school, there had been rules, and the first was of fraternity "between rich kids." Therefore, he was dumbfounded.

However, it is out of the question to throw in the towel: Joseph remained strong and kept on looking for work, even if it meant accepting small jobs that were unrelated to his qualifications. His guidelines were simple: he was to fight adverse circumstances; when these circumstances became too much, and under the right conditions, he was to go back to Le Cap with his wife and daughter.

News from Haiti was often confusing—disconcerting and reassuring—and put a strain on the young father's nerves. In this year 1909, the newspapers reported an attack perpetrated on the streetcar line in Port-au-Prince. The strange nature of the attack left Joseph perplexed.

It had all started with former minister Normil Sambour's anger. He was not happy because he wanted to come back to the government, as the position of Minister of Interior had been vacant since June 23, 1909. To win his case, he had a crazy idea—one that his supporters immediately implemented. Haitian newspaper *Le Matin*[134] reported that, one morning, they put on the streetcar rails, near the palace, a metal box containing explosive material. And when the streetcar came by, the bomb in question exploded. A few days later, another railway-related incident plunged the country into mourning: The special train carrying Antoine Simon, an ex-revolutionary who'd became president of the republic, hit a locomotive. There were eight deaths and fifteen injuries. The head of state was unscathed.

Finally, for Joseph, the only good news of the year 1909 was the return of Cincinnatus Leconte from exile. He was happy and relieved for

Cincinnatus's wife, Joseph's cousin Joséphine Laroche. But what Joseph did not know was that Cincinnatus was conspiring to seize power with the help of Joséphine. The plot took shape inside their residence in Le Cap, and the couple later sought support from some of the local agitators, "revolutionary farmers" known as the Cacos.[135] The armed insurrection, however, was quelled by the powers that be.

...

The suppression of the revolt was so ferocious that Cincinnatus Leconte's supporters either fled the country or went into hiding, while others were thrown into prison, including John Laroche, Joseph's cousin. "There were insistent rumors that they would shoot [the prisoners]," historian Marc Péan explains. "His Grace Kersuzan had to deploy all his ingenuity to save their lives. First, every night, he slept in a cot across from Le Cap prison. And once the prisoners were transferred to the capital, he went to Port-au-Prince where he stayed a long time, bothering Antoine Simon with his actions." Finally, John Laroche and the other prisoners were spared. Cincinnatus Leconte and his wife remained in hiding, as they waited for his moment to finally come. In Le Cap, they said that Joséphine Laroche could "galvanize her husband's ambition." In fact, if he one day got to power, she would be "the real Minister of Interior" of his government.

In 1909, another event almost went unnoticed: the mounting in February of the keel of a liner that would soon be talked about: the *France*. It belonged to the Compagnie Générale Transatlantique, and was not only the biggest French liner of the time, but the fastest as well, capable of a cruise speed of up to twenty-four-and-a-half knots. Built in Saint-Nazaire, the *France* had four chimneys and majestically spanned over a length of 217 meters. They'd nicknamed it the "Versailles of the Seas," with its classical decor, its Louis XIV salon style, and its dining room as tall as two decks, adorned with a mezzanine. As if on purpose, the keel of another liner, which would soon be talked about as well, was also mounted that same month: in the Belfast shipyard, the *Titanic* was taking shape. With its ten decks, it was even bigger than the *France*, but slightly slower: 269 meters long for a speed of twenty-four knots.

...

Far from the tumult surrounding the construction of the *Titanic* and the *France*, Joseph Laroche had a new reason to be happy. On July 2, 1910, a year and a half after the birth of Simone, the Laroches' second daughter, Louise, was born—in the family room, just like her older sister. Joseph felt the same excitement as the first time, although Louise was born prematurely, so that her fragile health required regular care and a fortune in medication. It was a problem for Joseph, who was not working or was working very little. Since he refused charity from his father-in-law, what could he do?

Once again, the answer came from Haiti. In May 1911, Cincinnatus Leconte set off again to conquer Haiti, once again assisted by Joséphine Laroche. This time, they were better prepared for the coup. The insurrection started in Le Cap and rapidly spread throughout the whole country, especially as President Antoine Simon was unanimously criticized. When the Cacos pushed back the army, it was President Simon's turn to flee. He went into exile while Cincinnatus Leconte triumphantly entered Port-au-Prince. On August 10, 1911, the deputies gathered and unanimously elected the new strongman of the country head of state. His wife, Joseph Laroche's cousin, demanded that she be called Queen Joséphine from now on.

Although Joseph Laroche might not have been interested in politics at first—he stayed away from intrigue for a long time—his family's ascent to power might have changed the game, particularly as he soon received an offer: two teaching positions at the secondary school in Le Cap, one in mathematics and the other one in physics. And, because when it rained, it poured, his mother was willing to pay for the tickets for the crossing of the couple with their children—an opportunity he couldn't refuse. When he approached Juliette with the opportunity, she was reluctant at first. She argued that her father, André Lafargue, was getting older and that she didn't want to abandon him; she argued that her whole life was in Villejuif; she argued that Haiti was unstable, with any situation on the verge of degeneration at any time. But Joseph could be patient and convincing. He succeeded in defusing his wife's fears and winning her approval. In the end, she agreed to follow him with Simone and Louise, telling herself that her husband had no future in France. Things would definitely be better in Le Cap.

Departure was set for the first part of 1912, and then was moved up when Joseph learned of Juliette's third pregnancy. He rushed to buy tickets on the *France*, whose maiden voyage was planned for April 20 from Le Havre. The plan was for the family to board another ship for Haiti once in New York—until Joseph Laroche discovered later that one of the *France's* rules forbade children from dining alongside their parents. He returned to the Compagnie Générale Transatlantique for a refund, and then headed to Rue Scribe, in Paris, to the office of the White Star Line, to purchase four tickets on the *Titanic*.

> **❝** When anyone asks how I can best describe my experience in nearly forty years at sea, I merely say, uneventful. Of course there have been winter gales, and storms and fog the like, but in all my experience, I have never been in any accident of any sort worth speaking about. [...] I never saw a wreck and never have been wrecked, nor was I ever in any predicament that threatened to end in disaster of any sort. You see, I am not very good material for a story. **❞**
> —Captain Smith, Commander of *Titanic*

. . .

On October 25, 1911, as Joseph Laroche was preparing for his departure, he received dire news: his cousin, Queen Joséphine, had just died in Le Cap. What a stroke of bad luck! She'd passed away just as her husband reached the Holy Grail they'd fought so hard for. Joseph was floored. After ten years of separation, he'd been so happy at the prospect of seeing his beloved cousin again. Fate had let him down.

The day after the funeral in Le Cap, the nation was mourning Mrs. Leconte. The front page of Haitian newspaper *Le Matin* described an atmosphere of great pain hovering on Queen Joséphine Leconte's native city. President Cincinnatus attended the ceremony in tears at Le Cap cathedral and then the burial at the city cemetery.

▪ ▪ ▪

Seven months later, as Joseph Laroche was on his way to Cherbourg to embark on the *Titanic* with Juliette, Simone, and Louise, he thought a lot of the departed family members: Joséphine, whom he would never see again, as well as Lisettine, who'd joined Uncle Bertrand in heaven. As their faces came back to him, Joseph wondered which childhood friends he would still find there. Had some of his classmates and neighbors stayed in Le Cap, or had they all left for other places—Port-au-Prince, New York, Mayence, or Paris? He had not exchanged letters with any of them during those nine years. In fact, when Joseph wanted to have news of any one of them, he'd asked his mother, who shared what she knew. He'd learned, for instance, that his schoolmate Luc Grimard, the orphan who could not finish secondary school, had become a teacher and journalist. What a twist of fate! Once, in January 1909, when things were difficult for Joseph in France, his mother had sent him an article from Luc Grimard. He was writing at the time for *Le Démocrate*,[136] one of Le Cap's newspapers. It had been a way for Euzélie to encourage her son to persevere. Grimard, three months older than he, had been treated harshly by life, only to overcome his situation. The article had impressed Joseph because it revealed both the informational style of the journalist, and the lyricism of the writer in him. The piece was about boats and read something like this: "It is 9:40. The French liner just anchored. It is drizzling. There is great animation around the decorated port. Rain showers are frequent. The Haitian flag above is like all souls: as it flutters, it does not feel the rain, but only wind and joy!"

FAMILY TREE

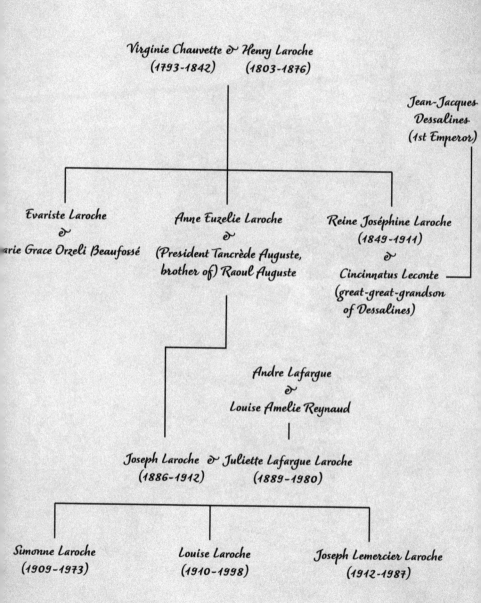

Virginie Chauvette & Henry Laroche
(1793-1842)   (1803-1876)

Jean-Jacques
Dessalines
(1st Emperor)

Evariste Laroche
&
Marie Grace Orzeli Beaufossé

Anne Euzelie Laroche
&
(President Tancrède Auguste,
brother of) Raoul Auguste

Reine Joséphine Laroche
(1849-1911)
&
Cincinnatus Leconte
(great-great-grandson
of Dessalines)

Andre Lafargue
&
Louise Amelie Reynaud

Joseph Laroche & Juliette Lafargue Laroche
(1886-1912)   (1889-1980)

Simonne Laroche
(1909-1973)

Louise Laroche
(1910-1998)

Joseph Lemercier Laroche
(1912-1987)

Name: Mr Joseph Philippe Lemercier Laroche
Titanic Victim
Born: Wednesday 26th May 1886
Age: 25 years 10 months and 20 days (Male)
Last Residence: in Paris, France
Occupation: Engineer
2nd Class Passengers
First Embarked: Cherbourg on Wednesday 10th April 1912
Ticket No. 2123, £41 11s 7d
Destination: Cap Haitien, Haiti
Died in the Titanic disaster (15th April 1912).
Body Not Recovered

Name: Mrs Juliette Marie Louise Laroche (née Lafargue)
Titanic Survivor
Born: Sunday 20th October 1889
Age: 22 years 5 months and 26 days (Female)
Marital Status: Married to Joseph
Last Residence: in Paris, France
2nd Class Passengers
First Embarked: Cherbourg on Wednesday 10th April 1912
Ticket No. 2123, £41 11s 7d
Destination: Cap Haitien, Haiti
Rescued (boat 14)
Disembarked Carpathia: New York City on Thursday 18th April 1912
Died: Thursday 10th January 1980 aged 90 years

Name: Miss Simonne Marie Anne Andrée Laroche
Titanic Survivor
Born: Friday 19th February 1909
Age: 3 years 1 month and 24 days (Female)
Last Residence: in Paris, France
2nd Class Passengers
First Embarked: Cherbourg on Wednesday 10th April 1912
Ticket No. 2123, £41 11s 7d
Destination: Cap Haitien, Haiti
Rescued (boat 14)
Disembarked Carpathia: New York City on Thursday 18th April 1912
Died: Wednesday 8th August 1973 aged 64 years

Name: Miss Louise Laroche
Titanic Survivor
Born: Saturday 2nd July 1910
Age: 1 years 9 months and 13 days (Female)
Last Residence: in Paris, France
2nd Class Passengers
First Embarked: Cherbourg on Wednesday 10th April 1912
Ticket No. 2123, £41 11s 7d
Destination: Cap Haitien, Haiti
Rescued (boat 14)
Disembarked Carpathia: New York City on Thursday 18th April 1912
Died: Sunday 25th January 1998 aged 87 years

The *Titanic* floating among icebergs on the water by cloudy day. 3D render.

"What do you think I am? Do you believe that I'm the sort that would have left that ship as long as there were any women and children on board? That's the thing that hurts, and it hurts all the more because it is so false and baseless. I have searched my mind with deepest care, I have thought long over each single incident that I could recall of that wreck. I'm sure that nothing wrong was done; that I did nothing that I should not have done. My conscience is clear and I have not been a lenient judge of my own acts."
—J. Bruce Ismay, Director of the White Star Line

"Control your Irish passions, Thomas. Your uncle here tells me you proposed sixty-four lifeboats and he had to pull your arm to get you down to thirty-two. Now, I will remind you just as I reminded him these are my ships. And, according to our contract, I have final say on the design. I'll not have so many little boats, as you call them, cluttering up my decks and putting fear into my passengers."
—J. Bruce Ismay, Director of the White Star Line

"You weren't there at my first meeting with Ismay. To see the little red marks all over the blueprints. First thing I thought was: 'Now here's a man who wants me to build him a ship that's gonna be sunk.' We're sending gilded egg shells out to sea."
—Thomas Andrews, Managing Director of Harland and Wolff Shipyards

"Let the Truth be known; no ship is unsinkable. The bigger the ship, the easier it is to sink her. I learned long ago that if you design how a ship'll sink, you can keep her afloat. I proposed all the watertight compartments and the double hull to slow these ships from sinking. In that way, you get everyone off. There's time for help to arrive, and the ship's less likely to break apart and kill someone while she's going down."
—Thomas Andrews, Managing Director of Harland and Wolff Shipyards

"The press is calling these ships unsinkable and Ismay's leadin' the chorus. It's just not true."
—Thomas Andrews, Managing Director of Harland and Wolff Shipyards

VII. Closer to You, My Lord

Another group of Haitians was also scheduled to board the Titanic in Cherbourg: The Mevs family and Mrs. Georges Labrousse. The Mevs did not make it, and Mrs. Labrousse arrived fifteen minutes late, and was extremely upset to find out that she would not be allowed to board the ship.

It was a dizzying feeling. Since boarding the *Titanic*, Joseph Laroche didn't know which way to turn. The spectacle was so mind-blowing that he had a hard time believing his eyes. Wherever he looked, there was luxury and majesty. He turned to Juliette, who turned to Simone: they were under the same spell. As for Louise, she was trying to take it all in, twisting and turning in her stroller when the elevator taking them to their cabin started rising. They hardly had a chance to discover their "apartment" and go into rapture over every little detail when it was time for dinner. In the huge dining room, it was hard to believe the second-class menu was less extravagant than that of the first class. There, twelve courses included two or three dishes each. Between the tapioca consommé, the spicy haddock, the curry chicken, the lamb with mint sauce, the peas, the turnip purée, the wine jelly, the American ice cream, the fresh fruit, and the cheese, the Laroches were in for a feast.

Joseph and Juliette Laroche joined Albert and Antonie Mallet. They had been inseparable since their meeting earlier that morning on the New York Express, the train from Saint-Lazare to Cherbourg; they'd transferred together to the *Nomadic*. During dinner, Joseph and Albert picked up where they'd left off two hours earlier. Now it was Joseph's turn to ask questions, which Albert Mallet gladly answered. He had the gift of gab. He was loquacious. It was a pleasure to listen to him.

Joseph asked him about his occupation as cognac merchant.

"I came into it by chance," Albert said. "I used to be a pharmacist. But that did not go as I wished. So, I left for Quebec and because I knew a bit about spirits, I applied and obtained the position. The work is pleasant. I meet a lot of people, and, in addition, it allows me to come back often to France."

"But how can you stand the cold?"

"They told me before I left that it was terrible and that I would not last very long. When I learned it could go down to −40 degree over there, I thought I would die. But, I withstood the first winter. The cold is not as dry as in France, and as long as you dress appropriately you will not have any problem."

How did he fit in? He laughed. "Everything goes well for a Frenchman, as long as he does not behave like a conqueror. Quebec used to be our home. It is no longer the case. If you understand that, and respect that, well, there will no difficulty at all."

Albert Mallet talked for almost half an hour. Only Joseph was listening to him, as Juliette and Antonie were feeding the children and having their own private conversation. At the end of the meal, the two families went back to their respective cabins, promising to meet again the next day.

For Joseph and Juliette Laroche, the journey could not have had a better start. They'd made friends with whom they could converse on this ship where everyone, or almost everyone, only spoke English.

Little Simone was also ecstatic, particularly as she had met, in addition to little André Mallet, other playmates. As for Louise, nobody was worried about her since, wherever they took her, she was always wriggling about in her stroller. This was a sign that all was well.

...

THE LAROCHE FAMILY

Joseph Laroche
05/26/1886-04/15/1912

Juliette Lafargue Laroche
10/20/1889-07/10/1980

Simonne Laroche
02/29/1909-08/08/1973

Louise Laroche
07/02/1910-01//25/1998

Joseph Lemercier Laroche
12/17/1912-01/17/1987

This is the dry dock that Titanic once sat, many years before its sinking. The
dock is located in Belfast, Northern Ireland.

At eight o'clock the next day, the waking was gentle. Everyone in the family had slept well. Not a tremor, not a rattle, had disturbed their pleasurable slumber.

"It's hard to believe we're on the ocean," Simone told her mother.

"Yes, but still make sure you don't run all over the place," her father said. He constantly kept an eye out.

After freshening up, they headed once again to the restaurant for an astounding array of breakfast choices, as overwhelming as the previous evening's meal. The second-class passengers were entitled to the best. The menu read: *Fruit. Oatmeal boiled corn. Fresh fish. Smoked herring. Beef kidneys and grilled bacon. Ground beef with potatoes. Grilled sausage, mashed potatoes. Grilled ham and fried eggs. French fries.*[137] *Pastries and Graham Rolls. Scones. Buckwheat cake,*[138] *maple syrup. Jam. Tea, coffee. Watercress.*

While at the restaurant, the Laroches learned that the ship was heading to Ireland for a last stopover before the great crossing. So, Juliette asked a crew member if she could give him a letter quickly, so the mail service could put it in the Irish post.

"Yes, Madame," he replied. She entrusted the children to Joseph and sat in a corner to write to her father. It was the letter that her daughter Louise would bring up during the Cherbourg ceremony in 1996:

> Dear Papa,
>
> I just learned that we will stop shortly. I am taking advantage of this fact to write you a few lines and give you news of us. We embarked on the Titanic last evening at 7:00 p.m. Oh, if only you could see this monster! Our tug looked like a fly next to it, and the interior could not be more comfortable. We have two bunks in our cabin, and the little girls are laying on a sofa turned into a bed, one at the head, the other at the foot, with a plank in the front so they will not fall. They are as well, if not better, than in their bed.
>
> The ship started up while we were dining, and we could not believe it was moving: it shakes less than the train. One hardly feels any

vibration. The girls ate well last evening. They slept in one stretch the whole night and were awoken by the bells announcing breakfast; those made Louise laugh.

Right now, they are walking on the covered deck with Joseph. Louise is in her small car, and Simone is pushing her. They have already made acquaintances: since Paris, we have traveled with a gentleman and a lady and their little boy, who is the same age as Louise. I believe they are the only French on board. So, we sit at the same table and like this we can chat.

Simone amused me earlier: she was playing with an English girl who had lent her a doll. My Simone was having great conversation, but the little girl could not understand anything. People are very nice on board. Yesterday, they were both running after a gentleman who had given them chocolate.

Juliette Laroche was not the only one amused by the mad chase performed by Simone and the English girl. A British passenger, Kate Buss,[139] echoed it as well in a letter she wrote to her family, mistaking the two girls for Asian passengers: "There are two absolutely lovely Japanese girls, about three or four years old, looking like dolls and running everywhere."

In another correspondence, Kate Buss described the pleasure she had listening to the *Titanic* orchestra, particularly the cellist, who smiled at her every time he finished a piece.

Coincidentally, in her letter to her father, Juliette Laroche also told of her joy while listening to classical music on the ship.

I am writing to you from the reading room, and an orchestra is playing next to me: one violin, two cellos, and one piano. I have not felt any sea sickness yet. I hope it will remain thus. The ocean is beautiful, and the weather is magnificent. If only you could see how big the ship is! One can hardly find his or her cabin in the succession of hallways.

Emigrants leaving Queenstown, Ireland, for New York, 1874.

Queenstown is a maritime town in Ireland, known as the *Titanic*'s last port of call. On April 11th, 1912, at 11:30 a.m., *Titanic* dropped the anchor in Queenstown. Tenders *Ireland* and *America* were waiting in the dock to transport 123 passengers out to board—sixty-three men and sixty women, for many of whom Queenstown was the gateway to a great new world. Of the 123 passengers that boarded in Queenstown, three were first class, seven were second class while the remaining 113 were third class (steerage). Just forty-four of the passengers that embarked from Queenstown survived.

The RMS *Titanic*.

Titanic Survivor: Denver Colorado socialite and woman's suffragist Margaret "Molly"Brown 1867-1932 ca.1900.

I am going to stop because I think we will stop over soon, and I would not like to miss the mail service. Thank you, again, dear Papa, for all your kindness. Please receive the best kisses from your daughter who loves you. Little Simone and Louise send big kisses to their good grandfather. After getting dressed this morning, they wanted to see you.

As Juliette finished her letter, Joseph continued to walk on the covered deck with the children. He was concerned. He had not known that the *Titanic* was to stop over in Ireland and, since he had been informed of it, he had been haunted by a brutal memory—one that had escaped him for at least fifteen years.

> **66** Just then the ship took a slight but definite plunge—probably a bulkhead went—and the sea came rolling along up in a wave, over the steel fronted bridge, along the deck below us, washing the people back in a dreadful huddled mass. Those that didn't disappear under the water right away, instinctively started to clamber up that part of the deck still out of water, and work their way towards the stern, which was rising steadily out of the water as the bow went down. It was a sight that doesn't bear dwelling on—to stand there, above the wheelhouse, and on our quarters, watching the frantic struggles to climb up the sloping deck, utterly unable to even hold out a helping hand. **99**
>
> —Charles Lightoller, Second Officer
> aboard *Titanic*

BELFAST, NI - JULY 14, 2016: Picture of constructors drawing plan in the
Titanic Belfast, visitor attraction dedicated to the RMS *Titanic*, a ship whic sank
by hitting an iceberg in 1912.

Sinking of the ocean liner the *Titanic* witnessed by survivors in lifeboats.
May 15, 1912.

After the sinking of the liner *Ville de Saint-Nazaire* in March 1897, survivor Marcel Héber-Suffrin had recounted the shipwreck victims' slog. The Martinican sailor had not stopped there, however. Aware of his luck for still being alive, he'd had also talked about his occupation and its dangers, evoking in particular another tragedy that had left its mark on him a few years earlier. In February 1886, the boat *Les Dix Frères*,[140] on which he had embarked, had endured a violent storm. "During the night, an infernal noise announced the fall of the main mast, after the shrouds had broken under the wind," he had recounted. "We were at the mercy of the winds." Soon the ship was nothing else but a "wreck" that was sinking slowly but surely, and on board, tension was at its height, especially as there was nothing left to eat, and two men had died.

Thinking despite himself about this story, Joseph Laroche felt goosebumps. He tried everything to block his memories and avoid remembering the end of the story, but Marcel Héber-Suffrin's voice inexorably resonated in his head. Joseph even visualized the gruesome scene—the one where the dead man was thrown into the sea.

No one ever claimed that the *Titanic* was "unsinkable." The quote, "practically unsinkable" was taken out of context. In 1911, *Shipbuilder* magazine published an article describing the construction of the *Titanic*. The article stated that when the watertight doors were closed, the ship would be "practically unsinkable."

"At dusk, around four, we washed the body," Héber-Suffrin had said. "These sepulchral ablutions consisted of a piece of fur wrapping the dead man strapped to a plank, with a pig mold at his feet. As I was the youngest, I was in charge of reciting the Pater Noster and the Ave Maria. We had tears in our eyes, as the dog was howling beside us. After the prayer, my companions lifted the plank and the body slumped into the sea. You can easily figure out what kind of night we had. And the ship was sinking lower. On the sixty-sixth day of this unforgettable adventure, a ship, having caught sight of our distress signals, sent its boat. The ocean was still very rough. It was March 20. On April 1 we were disembarking in Queenstown, Ireland, from where the French consul sent us back to Le Havre and Martinique."

Queenstown. The word brought him shivers. It was precisely in Queenstown that the *Titanic* was to stop over shortly. Joseph Laroche could not shake the apprehension that had taken over him, angry at himself for remembering Héber-Suffrin's long-forgotten and foreboding tale. He vigorously shook his head to chase away the gloomy thoughts and smiled at Louise, who was waving at him from her stroller.

▪ ▪ ▪

Queenstown, a maritime town, had a long history with ships, so that it often made the news. The first steamboat connecting Ireland to England had left from its port in 1821. The first steamboat to have crossed the Atlantic in 1838 had departed from there. The town was called Cobh until 1849, when Queen Victoria herself came to visit her subjects. In the general euphoria, Cobh was renamed Queenstown, before going back to its original name after Ireland gained independence in 1921.

But on April 11, 1912, when the *Titanic* arrived in Queenstown at 11:30 a.m., poverty undermined and exhausted Ireland, so much so that many of its inhabitants only had one thing in mind: leave at any cost for a chance at a better life elsewhere. Irish people were willing to cross the Atlantic to find happiness in the United States or Canada. This was the case for Millvina Dean's family, for instance, an Englishwoman Louise Laroche would later meet in Paris, in July 2005. Millvina's father had chosen to migrate to Kansas with his wife, Eva Georgette, his two-month-old daughter Millvina, and his two-year-old son, Bertram. Once in the United States, he intended to open a tobacco store. In search of the American dream, the family traveled in third class, like most of the 119 Irish passengers who boarded the *Titanic* at the Queenstown stopover. On board the sea giant, these determined immigrants promised themselves that they would start a new life at the other side of the ocean.

66 The sounds of people drowning are something
that I cannot describe to you, and neither can
anyone else. It's the most dreadful sound and
there is a terrible silence that follows it. **99**

—Eva Hart, Titanic *survivor*

At 1:30 p.m., as the newcomers settled, the ship cast off! The contrast was striking between the immigrants who were leaving to find work in America, for lack of it at home, and Joseph Laroche, who was going back home, where he'd gotten a life-changing offer that had been unavailable in France. But, as the ship moved away from the Irish coast, a thousand questions hit the Haitian engineer. Would he find his way around in the city of Le Cap, which he had he left eleven years before? So much had happened during his absence. As a matter of fact, he had changed as well: the twenty-five-year-old man he was today, with his large mustache, did not have a lot in common with the fifteen-year-old, smooth-faced and innocent boy who'd departed from Haiti in 1901. Furthermore, now he was married. It would be his wife's turn to be a stranger on his island. Would she be welcome and accepted, and would she fit in? More specifically, how would it be for her to live with Euzélie, with whom he had a special relationship? Would his mother continue to treat him like a child, refusing to see that he had grown up? Would she be jealous of Juliette?

While Joseph Laroche pondered these questions, he nevertheless felt happy to go home. He already felt them: all the vibrations of Le Cap rising inside of him. He was overwhelmed by joy on the deck of the *Titanic*, where he had been walking with his daughters for an hour.

L'Institution du Saint-Esprit.

On July 21st, 1912, two months after this requiem mass, Joseph Laroche's memory was revived again, one hundred kilometers away, at the school in Beauvais, when the alumni association of Institution du Saint-Esprit held their yearly general assembly.

"You can take a Haitian from Haiti, but you cannot take Haiti from a Haitian," his mother often said, before he'd left, to help him withstand all seasons in France. This made him smile because it had been proven true by experience. He looked at Simone and Louise. He was also happy that his daughters would get to know Le Cap. In Le Cap, nobody would bother them for what they were, because race-mixing was anchored into the country's DNA. In Le Cap, they would have enough space to run as they pleased. In Le Cap, he would put them to bed with new stories of Bouki, Anansi, or Brother Rabbit that he'd learn as soon as he arrived.

On the *Titanic*, even the smoking room reminded Joseph of his homeland. Only men gathered there, playing cards and chess, but also dominoes. Ah, dominoes! It was the game *par excellence* in Haiti—one of observation, attention, and tactics. In Le Cap, the games were endless. The elders put the pieces down with a thud, slamming them on the wooden table. Some were very shrewd, just like in the folktales of his childhood. When they realized that their opponent was about to block them, they caused an incident on purpose, like spilling a bottle of rum, and this caused confusion or interrupted the game. When Joseph thought about it, he couldn't help laughing by himself. He liked dominoes for the atmosphere it created, as well as for the pleasure it gave him as a mathematician. In fact, he told himself, why not use that game to enhance the students' skills in numbers, calculation, and problem-solving? It was something to consider. He would talk about it with his colleagues teaching in lower grades.

■ ■ ■

Sunday, April 14, 1912. Three days had gone by since the last stopover in Ireland. Finely dressed, Joseph took his family to mass, a gathering he would not miss for anything in the world, even at sea. Since his First Communion in Le Cap, he had liked going to church, for the biblical readings, the priest's lectures, and the atmosphere. On the *Titanic*, the service took place in the second-class living room and was presided over by Father Thomas Byles,[141] a British vicar on his way to Brooklyn to celebrate his brother's wedding. Father Montvila,[142] a Lithuanian priest, and Father Peruschitz, a German priest joined him as he delivered his sermon in English and then in French. Father Thomas Byles reminded the assembly that "man needs religious comfort as a rescue boat, within easy reach in case of spiritual sinking." As Father Peruschitz[143] took his turn to preach in German and in Hungarian, a strange feeling overtook Joseph. He'd never once imagined he would be on a boat, listening to a homily. He considered it a "blessing" for the rest of the day, particularly as it was sunny outside. He was grateful that Juliette was happy, that Louise was smiling, and that Simone was having a blast with the English girl.

At 6:00 p.m., dinner was served with, as usual, an appetizing menu. The Laroches and Mallets met again and then went back to their respective cabins.

But soon...tragedy struck.

. . .

In the middle of the night, a steward burst into the cabin, shaking Joseph and Juliette awake. "You need to hurry," he said in English. "The liner hit an iceberg. You must put on life jackets and go up on the deck."

In half a second, Joseph understood the situation. As he took Louise in his arms, many of his childhood memories resurfaced—all about the many sinkings that had troubled his mind. He thought of the *Santa Maria*, of the *Ville de Saint-Nazaire*, of the *Saint-Guillaume*. He calmly explained the situation to Juliette and asked her to go ahead of him with Simone and follow the steward. In a moment like this, Joseph knew, each minute counts. He gathered all the family's money, valuables and paperwork, and slid them into his jacket pockets, before wrapping Louise in that same jacket. He then ran after Juliette and Simone, while panic ensued among many of the passengers. Once on the deck, in the middle of the melee, Joseph Laroche clung to a sailor separating men from women. Holding Louise tight, he desperately scanned for Juliette and Simone. He finally caught sight of them.

The rest was told by Juliette.

When the collision happened, there was terrible panic. People were pushing, in a hurry to get off the boat. Suddenly, I felt that they were pulling my older daughter away from me, my little Simone...I saw her thrown to a lifeboat suspended above the abyss. "My child," I yelled. "My child! It is my child that was taken away!"

But right at that instant, I felt someone grabbing me as well. A pair of hands took me, and threw me into emptiness. I found myself in the lifeboat, next to my little Simone, and up there, on the deck, in the middle of the scramble, I glimpsed my husband. Arms extended above the crowd, he was holding our younger girl, whom he was trying to protect against the push. He was struggling against the sailors, showing them the little girl and trying to make them understand that she was separated from me, her mother. At last someone grabbed our little Louise from my husband's hands, and soon she was in my arms.

Then the lifeboat was once and for all lowered onto the sea. I hardly had time to bid my husband a final farewell. I heard his voice, above the rumble, yelling: "See you soon, darling! There will be space for everyone, don't worry, in the lifeboats...Take care of our girls...See you soon!"

And the lifeboat moved away...

■ ■ ■

His wife and daughters in the lifeboats, Joseph Laroche was waiting for his turn, standing in the middle of the ghost ship the *Titanic* had turned into. They told him, and the other passengers still on board, that boats would arrive shortly to rescue them. But time was passing by—half an hour, an hour, and then two—and the ship was taking on more water. Hope was fading. But what could one do, other than keep the faith until the end? Although filled with fear, Joseph Laroche told himself that a miracle was always possible. He thought about the Martinican survivor of the *Ville de Saint-Nazaire* who'd been saved *in extremis* by a passing boat.

> 66 About this time people began jumping from
> the stern, my friend Milton Long and myself
> stood beside each other and jumped on the rail.
> We did not give each other any messages for
> back home 'cause neither thought we would
> ever get back. 99
> —Jack B. Thayer, Titanic *survivor*

He went back to the living room where the morning mass had been held. In this makeshift chapel, Father Byles was praying "with Catholics, Protestants and Jews kneeling all around him." He had refused to embark on a lifeboat when they had offered him the opportunity, as he wanted to comfort the passengers who remained on board. He, Father Montvila and Father Peruschitz were hearing confessions and giving absolution, and the scene made Joseph Laroche emotional. He automatically joined the group, while the orchestra was tirelessly playing a melody he recognized; he had heard it fifteen years before, when he'd attended his Uncle Bertrand's funeral at the small cemetery in Le Cap. He had not forgotten that hymn, the farewell song that had touched him so, and sent a chill down his spine:

My God closer to You
Closer to You
It is the cry of my faith
Closer to You

Suddenly, the music stopped. A great silence settled on the *Titanic,* followed by a huge crash. A chimney suddenly fell, crushing passengers under its weight. This reignited the panic. As some people jumped to the sea, other held on tightly to whatever they could find: banisters, chairs, rails. The water rushed in from everywhere. The hull broke in two pieces, and the front of the ship was abruptly submerged. The last lights went off.

The *Titanic* sank.

This time, it was the end. Joseph Laroche cried out, petrified. All was clear in his mind. He thought of Juliette, of Simone and Louise, of Euzélie and Le Cap.

He would never see Haiti again.

. . .

❝ I was only seven, but I remember thinking that everything in the world was standing still. **❞**
—Eva Hart, Titanic *survivor*

In New York, where she disembarked with her daughters, the news of Joseph's death devastated Juliette Laroche. She was in shock, distressed, and desperate. As she went from holding onto hope to facing the dramatic reality, she knew that her life would never be the same again. At twenty-two, she was a widow with no financial resources, with two children and another on the way. The money and jewelry that Joseph had hidden in the jacket covering Louise had been stolen on the *Carpathia*, the ship that had rescued them. But what pained Juliette the most was that her wedding band was missing. Since when? she wondered. She couldn't remember exactly. She had entrusted the ring to Joseph because she had lost a lot of weight at the beginning of her pregnancy, and it was constantly sliding off. At the moment they separated on the *Titanic*, Joseph had either put it back on her finger, or buried it in the jacket. Anyway, she no longer had this memento.

On their descent from the *Carpathia,* the Laroche and Mallet families were transferred to Saint-Vincent Hospital for a week, during which Juliette received care for frostbite. The pain was horrible, as her feet had remained immersed in the freezing water for long hours in the lifeboat. After her release, Juliette moved with Simone and Louise into a big hotel, thanks to a generous American woman who took charge of them and bought them new clothes. Three weeks after the sinking, the French newspaper *Le Matin* dedicated an article to Juliette, Simone, and Louise Laroche's return to France. The liner *Chicago*,[144] which took them back to France from New York, berthed at 9:30 a.m. in Le Havre harbor on May 2, 1912. A correspondent of the daily newspaper was present. He wrote:

> *At the arrival of the liner, you could notice an old man in mourning clothes looking anxiously at the disembarking passengers on the dock. It was Mrs. Laroche's father, who had come to Paris to welcome his daughter and two granddaughters for their sad return to French soil. When Mrs. Laroche and her two daughters appeared on the gangway, the old man ran to them and father and daughter hugged for a long time, teary-eyed. Mrs. Laroche then recounted that at the time of the catastrophe, she and her two little girls had been forced to leave her husband behind. He'd tried to reassure her, affirming that he would be rescued just like her—only a little later. Crying, the poor woman repeated several times: "I believed him! I believed him! Otherwise, I would have never agreed to leave him!"*

> **“** At 8:30 all the people were on board. I wanted to hold a service, a short prayer of thankfulness for those rescued and a short burial service for those who were lost. While they were holding the service, I maneuvered around the scene of the wreckage. We saw nothing but one body. **”**
> —Captain Arthur H. Rostron, Commander of *Carpathia*

...

In Le Cap, Euzélie was just as overcome. She remained motionless, incredulous, destroyed. Her only son was dead—the one she'd loved so much, and whose brilliant future she'd seen to. She would never embrace him again. The entire Laroche family stood together with her. What a cruel irony! She was crying about the departure of the one person whose return they'd been ready to celebrate. However, they saluted with pride "the heroic and gallant behavior" of Euzélie's son.

. . .

Joseph Laroche's body would never be found, unlike dozens of others recovered by ships dispatched to the spot a few days later by the White Star Line.

For Juliette Laroche, who was back at her father's house with her daughters, it started a painful ordeal. How could one grieve without seeing a loved one for the last time? In an attempt at closure, on Friday May 24, 1912, at 10:00 a.m., at the Villejuif church, Juliette Laroche invited family and friends to a "service for the repose of the soul of Mr. Joseph Laroche." The death announcement included the names of the highest Haitian political and military figures of the time, uncles and cousins of the departed: President Cincinnatus Leconte, Ambassador Nemours Auguste, Senator Déjoie Laroche, Public Works Secretary John Laroche, as well as General François Beaufossé Laroche and General Timoléon Laroche.

A huge crowd attended the ceremony in a moving French-Haitian communion. To all, Juliette distributed a souvenir card with a picture of her husband framed with a black band. The reverse side read: "Please pray for the repose of the soul of Joseph Laroche, who passed away on April 15, 1912, in the sinking of the *Titanic.*" The words were simple for this ultimate farewell to the departed engineer, and the tears were abundant.

In two days, Joseph Laroche would have turned twenty-six years old.

On July 21, 1912, two months after this requiem mass, Joseph Laroche's memory was revived again, one hundred kilometers away, at the school in Beauvais, when the alumni association of Institution du Saint-Esprit held their yearly general assembly. In front of sixty or so attendees, Abbot

Dupuis, the school superior, evoked their schoolmate's "tragic end": "He was at the Institution for three years," he said, "and his pleasant character had gained him everyone's liking. He was among those brave people who stayed on the boat, after having embraced what was dearest to them. It is impossible to think without intense emotion of these hours full of anguish during which, in the cold night darkness, the shipwrecked waited for the rescue that was not coming; of this tragic instant when the huge mass of the ship went down into the water."

. . .

On August 8, 1912, a new tragedy hit the Laroche family. Joseph's uncle, President Cincinnatus Leconte, also met a tragic end, inside the presidential palace in Port-au-Prince. Many later said that the two men's destinies had been connected. The Haitian media stirred: "This morning, around 3:25, a horrible explosion woke the whole of the population. The formidable detonation was accompanied with the noise of hails of bullets. The palace had just been blown up. Gigantic flames scattered a red light on a whole part of the city," the daily newspaper *Le Matin* reported.

The country wondered whether it had been an accident or, rather, a planned attack. Some described the mass of "smoking ruins" found where the remains of Cincinnatus Leconte, two members of the Laroche family, and about two hundred soldiers lay. The survivors, among them Public Works State Secretary John Laroche, Joseph's cousin, rapidly provided details on the tragedy. "I was abruptly pulled from sleep by the sound of a big detonation," Leconte explained. "When I opened my eyes, the sky was above me. I wasn't feeling any shock. I don't remember falling. My first thought was to run to the president's room. That room no longer existed."

The parallel between President Cincinnatus Leconte's and his nephew's "tragic end" become even more striking as testimonies were gathered. Both men confronted death, one at sea and the other on land, in the same conditions: they were alone and powerless in the face of what was forthcoming. *Le Matin* reported that "President Leconte's charred remains were found where the floor had collapsed. Immobilized from the first moments and buried under rubble, the president could only think of his family and, resigned to his end, encourage the others to flee for their lives."

A few hours after the explosion, the National Assembly met and elected Tancrède Auguste, Joseph Laroche's paternal uncle, the new President of the Republic. Power stayed in the family. In fact, for his first official visit, Tancrède Auguste went to Le Cap on December 11, 1912. He was feverishly welcomed as he toured the city on horseback. In the evening, a great ball, "illuminated by electricity," was given at the market.

■ ■ ■

On December 17, 1912, far from Haitian reality, a happy event occurred in Villejuif. Eight months after the sinking of the *Titanic*, Juliette Laroche gave birth to a boy. She named him Joseph to honor her late husband.

But, behind the joy brought by the newborn, the pain persisted. Furthermore, the family had a hard time making ends meet. André Lafargue's business was not doing as well as before. The situation worsened two years later with the outbreak of World War I. Juliette's father then urged her to claim compensation from the White Star Line, and she eventually did. In 1918, the American company paid Juliette Laroche 150,000 francs for damages. She immediately opened a dry-cleaning business in one of the rooms in her father's house. Finally, after years of stress, the family could breathe financially and contemplate the future with confidence.

In 1920, Euzélie Laroche came to France to meet her daughter-in-law and grandchildren whom she had never seen. She stayed three months in Villejuif, and then went back to Le Cap, where she resumed her Kay-Kafé business and her speculator activities. She also took care of the little orphan, Carlet Auguste, Joseph's half-brother. Historian Georges Michel explained that, after Joseph Laroche's death, Zélie had transferred all her maternal love to young Carlet, who was the son of a man she had loved. So, almost every day after school, Carlet went to Euzélie's Kay-Kafé ,where he got sweets, coffee, chocolate, fruit, and money.

However, whether in Haiti or in France, life was no longer the same for Joseph Laroche's mother, wife, and children. His absence was cruel in its permanence—insurmountable. It haunted them, and it was a burden of which they would never be free.

. . .

In 1952, Euzélie passed away in Le Cap.

In 1973, Simone's death in Villejuif followed.

In 1980, Juliette, who never remarried, died. The tomb of the Haitian engineer's widow still bears the inscription: "Juliette Laroche 1889–1980, wife of Joseph Laroche, missing at sea from the RMS *Titanic* since April 15, 1912."

In 1987, Laroche Jr. died.

In 1998, Louise Laroche joined them all.

Acknowledgments

I would like to thank the descendants of Joseph Laroche for the privilege of interviewing them, particularly Christina Schutt, the great-grandniece of Joseph Laroche, who not only provided letters and other written materials, but also shared her family's oral history.

Thanks to Georges Michel, who helped with my research immensely; to Christian Boutillier, who shared with me a file that documented the everyday life at École du Saint-Esprit in Beauvais; and to Bruno Rousseau, who helped me revive my own memories of boarding school life and allowed me to walk in Joseph Laroche's shoes.

I'm also thankful to François Codet, who gave me access to the archives of the French Titanic Society; to Father Roger Tabard, who allowed me to consult the archives of Congrégation du Saint-Esprit; and to Myriam Sylvain, who generously introduced me to Gaétan Mentor from the Haitian Historical Society.

Thank you to the Haitian Historical Society.

Thank you to Carline Duverseau, who introduced me to Mango.

To the good people at Mango: I appreciate your tremendous support and dedication. Chris, Hugo, Robin, and Morgane, you are all wonderful!

To M.J. Fievre, editor extraordinaire: Un grand merci.

SERGE BILÉ

Bibliography

Chapter I

Audio excerpt from JT soir / France 3 in Basse Normandie, dated April 19, 1996.

Chérubini, Nadine and Franck Gavard-Perret. "Harold S. Bride: une étude." *The French Titanic Association: Latitudes 41*, no. 46 (2010).

Codet, François, Olivier Mendez, Alain Dufief, and Franck Gavard-Perret. *Les Français du Titanic*. Rennes: Marines éditions, 2011.

La Chaîne Météo. "Les chroniques météos de 1912." Accessed December 27, 2018. http://www.meteoparis.com/chronique/annee/1912.

La Patrie. "Histoire touchante de deux petits rescapés" Apr. 22, 1912.

La Presse de la Manche. "En souvenir du Titanic." April 1996.

Le Matin. "Une rescapée du Titanic." May 3, 1912.

Mendez, Olivier. "Louise Laroche, la dernière demoiselle française." *The French Titanic Association: Latitudes 41*, no. 1 (1998).

Mendez, Olivier. "Quelques souvenirs personnels de Millvina Dean." *The French Titanic Association: Latitudes 41*, no. 43.

"The Real Café Parisien." *The Shipbuilder* (1912).

Chapter II

Benoît, Joachim, "Commerce et décolonisation: L'expérience franco-haïtienne au XIXe siècle." *Annales: Économies, Sociétés, Civilisations*, 27th year, no. 6 (1972): 1497–1525.

Dauphin, Claude, "Le conte chanté comme lieu d'accumulation d'un savoir musical." *Yearbook of the International Folk Music Council*, vol. 12 (1981): 77–83.

Deleage, Paul. *Haï"ti en 1886.* Paris: Édition Dentu, 1887.

Homepage of Jan Henri Cocatre-Zilgien, "Marcel Héber-Suffrin." Accessed December 27, 2018. http://www.cocatrez.net/MarcelHeberSuffrin/index.html.

INESA. *Le café en Haïti.* September 2001.

Michel, Georges (historian), in discussion with the author. September 2014.

Péan, Marc. *L'illusion héroïque 1890–1902, 25 ans de vie capoise.* Port-au-Prince: Henry Deschamps, 1977.

Schutt, Christina (descendant of Joseph Laroche), in discussion with the author. September 2014.

Schutt, Christina, "Les actes d'État civil du Cap." *Genèse: Journal généalogique et historique,* December 27, 2018. http://www.agh.qc.ca/articles/?id=26.

Chapter III

Auguste, Carlet R. *Projections sur l'économie d'Haïti.* Port-au-Prince: Éditions Fardin, 1983.

Chaibi, Khalid. Oumma. "Aimé Césaire: Il est bien plus difficile d'être un homme libre que d'être un esclave." Accessed December 27, 2018. https://oumma.com/aime-cesaire-il-est-bien-plus-difficile-detre-un-homme-libre-que-detre-un-esclave/.

Clorméus, Lewis Ampidu. "*État, religions et politique* en Haïti (XVIIIe–XXIe siècles)." *Karthala: Histoire, Monde, et Cultures religieuses* no. 29 (2014).

de Molinari, Gustave. *À Panama: l'isthme de Panama—la Martinique—Haïti.* Paris: Guillaumin et Cie, 1886.

de Wimpffen, Alexandre-Stanislas. *Haïti au XVIIIe siècle: Richesse et esclavage dans une colonie française.* Paris: Karthala, 1993.

Frisch, Peter J. "L'état civil de Port-au-Prince, témoin du massacre général des Blancs." *G.H.C.* no. 58 (1994): 1005.

Jan, Mgr J. M. *Diocèse du Cap Haï¨tien. Un siècle d'histoire 1860–1960.* Port-au-Prince: Henri Deschamps, 1959.

Péan, Marc. *Vingt-cinq ans de vie capoise, Volume I (L'illusion héroïque).* Port-au-Prince: Henri Deschamps, 1977.

Péan, Marc. *Vingt-cinq ans de vie capoise, Volume III (La ville éclatée).* Port-au-Prince: Imprimeur II, 1993.

Turnier, Alain. *Les États-Unis et le marché haïtien.* Washington, 1955.

Vandercook, John W. *Majesté noire.* Paris: Firmin-Didot, 1930.

Chapter IV

Airiau, Paul. "'Trois collèges spiritains en France à la fin du XIXe siècle: *Épinal*, Merville, Beauvais." *Mémoire Spiritaine* no. 20 (2004).

Desquiron, Jean. *Haïti à la une, une anthologie de la presse haïtienne de 1724 à 1934.* Port-au-Prince: S.N. 1995.

Institution du Saint-Esprit de Beauvais, "1900–1901 School Directory."

Jean Ernoult. *Histoire de la province spiritaine de France.* (Congrégation du Saint-Esprit, 2000).

Mouchard, Abbé. "L'Enseignement chrétien." *Revue d'enseignement secondaire* (1921).

Newsletters of the Congrégation du Saint-Esprit, de 1850 à 1920 (Archives of the parent company in Chevilly-Larue).

Rouger, Michel. "Entre les Bretons et Haï¨ti une si longue histoire." *Place publique* no. 5 (2010).

Société d'Histoire Moderne. "Race, couleur et indépendance en Haïti (1804–1825)." *Revue d'histoire moderne* Tome XXV (April–June 1978).

Chapter V

Airiau, Paul. "Trois collèges spiritains en France à la fin du XIXe siècle: *Épinal*, Merville, Beauvais." *Mémoire Spiritaine* no. 20 (2004).

Ernoult, Jean. *Histoire de la province spiritaine de France*. Paris: Congrégation du Saint-Esprit, 2000.

Frossard, Marcel. *La maison natale d'Alexandre Dumas*. Accessed December 27, 2018. http://cfranquelin.free.fr/shrvc/production/ maison_natale_pages_de_1961_1962_tome_08.pdf.

Institution du Saint-Esprit de Beauvais, "1900–1901 School Directory."

Jey, Martine. Fabula. "Gustave Lanson et la réforme de 1902: Défense d'une réforme, compromis, et décalage." Accessed December 27, 2018. https://www.fabula.org/atelier.php?Gustave_Lanson_et_ la_r%26eacute%3Bforme_de_1902.

Newsletters of the Congrégation du Saint-Esprit, de 1850 à 1920 (Archives of the parent company in Chevilly-Larue).

Chapter VI

Chancrin, Ernest and Rémi Dumont. *Larousse agricole: encyclopédie illustrée, Volume 1*. Paris: Larousse, 1921.

Codet, François and Olivier Mendez, Alain Dufief, Franck Gavard-Perret. *Les Français du Titanic*. Rennes: Marines éditions, 2011.

Desquiron, Jean. *Haïti à la une, une anthologie de la presse haïtienne de 1724 à 1934*. Port-au-Prince: S.N. 1995.

Fontaine, Astrid. *Le peuple des tunnels*. Paris: Ginkgo éditeur, 2013.

L'illustration. "Le tunnel du métropolitain sous la Seine." November 25, 1905.

Le Nouvelliste. "La route jamaïcaine de Jean Victor Généus." August 21, 2014.

Marchand, Philippe. *Histoire de Lille.* Paris: Éditions Jean-Paul Gisserot, 2009.

Mendez, Olivier. "Miss Louise Laroche." *The Titanic Commutator,* Volume 19, no. 2 (August–October 1995).

Patard, Frédéric. *Presse de la manche.* "Cherbourg port du Titanic et des transats" (2011).

Péan, Marc. *Vingt-cinq ans de vie capoise, Volume III (La ville éclatée).* Port-au-Prince: Imprimeur II, 1993.

Pourprix, Marie-Thérèse. "Les mathématiques à la Faculté des Sciences de Lille et leur ouverture au monde socio-économique (1854–1970)" in the minutes of the September 15, 2011, meeting of the alumni association of the Université Lille.

Robinet, René. Conseil général du département du Nord. "Introduction aux notices relatives aux recteurs de l'académie de Douai-Lille de 1809 à 1940." *Répertoire numérique de la série T-Enseignement 1800–1940, Sous-Série 2T Fonds du rectorat de Douai-Lille* (1991).

Schutt, Christina (descendant of Joseph Laroche), in discussion with the author. September 2014.

Chapter VII

Codet, François and Olivier Mendez, Alain Dufief, Franck Gavard-Perret. *Les Français du Titanic.* Rennes: Marines éditions, 2011.

Desquiron, Jean. *Haïti à la une, une anthologie de la presse haïtienne de 1724 à 1934.* Port-au-Prince: S.N. 1995.

Geller, Judith B. *Titanic, Women and Children First.* Cambridge: Patrick Stephens, 1998.

Homepage of Jan Henri Cocatre-Zilgien, "Marcel Héber-Suffrin." Accessed December 27, 2018. http://www.cocatrez.net/MarcelHeberSuffrin/index.html.

Le Matin. "Rescapée du Titanic: Ce que dit Madame Laroche." May 2, 1912.

Le Matin. "Une rescapée du Titanic." May 3, 1912.

Michel, Georges. *Le Nouvelliste.* "L'ambassadeur Carlet R. Auguste et le Titanic." Sept. 10, 2001.

Newsletters of the Congrégation du Saint-Esprit, de 1850 à 1920 (Archives of the parent company in Chevilly-Larue).

About the Author

Ivorian-French writer Serge Bilé is the author of several essays and documentaries about the Black and Caribbean experience. Over 100,000 copies of his book *The Blacks in Nazi Camps* have been sold worldwide. Currently, he is a news anchorman for Martinique Première, a network of France Télévision group and the most watched TV newscaster on prime time on the island.

A prolific author, Serge Bilé has authored or coauthored over a dozen books, including *Noirs dans les camps nazis* (Éditions Serpent à plumes, 2005), *La légende du sexe surdimensionné des Noirs* (Éditions Serpent à plumes, 2005), *Sur le dos des hippopotames* (Éditions Calmann-Lévy, 2006), *Tiwa et la pierre miroir* (Édition Monde Global, 2006), *Quand les Noirs avaient des esclaves blancs* (Pascal Galodé Éditeurs, 2008), *Le miracle oublié* (Pascal Galodé Éditeurs, 2008), *Et si Dieu n'aimait pas les Noirs?* (Pascal Galodé Éditeurs, 2008), *Au secours, le prof est noir!* (Pascal Galodé Éditeurs, 2009), *Blanchissez-moi tous ces nègres* (Pascal Galodé Éditeurs, 2010), *Sombres Bourreaux* (Pascal Galodé Éditeurs, 2012), *La Mauresse de Moret* (Pascal Galodé Éditeurs, 2012), and *Singe, les dangers de la bananisation des esprits* (Dagan Éditions, 2013).

Endnotes

1   **Cherbourg-Octeville:** The second largest man-made harbor in the world at the time, Cherbourg-Octeville, in the northwest of France, was the first stop on the *Titanic's* maiden voyage. *Titanic* arrived in Cherbourg in the late afternoon. Two tenders, *Nomadic* and *Traffic*, transported 281 passengers from the dock to the fated liner which was moored in Cherbourg's harbor. The dock was later renamed after an American General by the name of Lawton-Collins whose men freed Cherbourg during World War II. In Cherbourg, a plaque was unveiled by Louise Laroche in memory of the passengers who'd boarded the RSM *Titanic*.

2   **Louise Laroche:** Louise Laroche was a second-class passenger of the *Titanic* who survived the sinking. She boarded the Titanic at Cherbourg-Octeville with her father Joseph, mother Juliette and sister Simonne. Joseph died in the sinking but his family was saved, in either lifeboat no. 8 or lifeboat no. 14. Louise Laroche never married. She died in Villejuif, France, on January 25, 1998 at age 89, shortly after James Cameron's movie, *Titanic*, came out.

3   **Lawton-Collins:** J. Lawton-Collins was a US Army commander who was nicknamed "Lightning Joe" and became a hero at Guadalcanal and Normandy. He was one of the few American soldiers to have served in both the Pacific and European Theaters of Operations. He's been quoted, saying, "No matter how brilliant a man may be, he will never engender confidence in his subordinates and associates if he lacks simple honesty and moral courage." His nephew, Michael Collins, piloted the famous Apollo 11 space mission that transported two men to the moon.

4   **Renault AG1s:** To get from Paris to Cherbourg-Octeville, the Laroche family hired two Renault AGs that started with crank handles. The

AG1 (Taxi de la Marne) was the first car produced after Marcel Renault's death in 1903. It used a taximeter, a relatively new invention that automatically calculated how much the passenger had to pay. According to the *Renaud Classic* website, "Taxi service provided valuable exposure for the Renault name and brought it recognition beyond France. In 1907, Renault sold 1,100 units in London." The name Taxi de la Marne was not used until the outbreak of World War I, when 1,300 taxis were requisitioned by the French Army to transport 6,000 soldiers from Paris to the First Battle of the Marne in early September 1914.

5   **Villejuif:** The Laroche family lived in Villejuif, a commune in the southern suburbs of Paris, France, about a dozen kilometers from the Saint-Lazare train station. Villejuif means "Jewtown," but there is no record of medieval Jews having lived in Villejuif. Jewish-language columnist Philologos questions the origins of the name: "And what about the fact that, *ville* being grammatically feminine, 'Jewtown' should have been *Villejuive* and not *Villejuif*? Was the 'v' devoiced into an 'f' over time? Was the original name *ville des juifs* or *ville aux juifs,* 'the town of the Jews,' from which the *des* (of) or *aux* (pertaining or belonging to) was eventually dropped?"

6   **Haitian Creole:** Haitian Creole is a French-based creole language spoken by ten to twelve million people worldwide. The language developed from contact between French settlers and African slaves during the Atlantic slave trade in Haiti. It was also influenced by Portuguese, Spanish, English, Taino, and West African languages. Joseph Laroche used the Creole language to scold his children. Even if Louise and Simone did not speak Creole, they understood its urgency and obeyed immediately, although without fear.

7   **New York Express:** The *New York Express* was a luxury train that could go up to 56 mph or 90 kph.

8 **John Jacob Astor:** John Jacob "Jack" Astor IV (1864–1912) was a wealthy American businessman, a prominent member of the Astor family, and the first multimillionaire in the US. He traveled with his wife on the opulent New York Express to the *Nomadic* and died in the early hours of the sinking of the *Titanic*. He was the richest passenger aboard and was believed to have been one of the wealthiest men in the world at that time. **Interesting anecdote:** A charity once called Astor for a possible contribution, a request he responded to by donating fifty dollars. When being told by a disappointed committee, "Oh, Mr. Astor, your son William gave us a hundred dollars," he replied, "Yes, but you must remember that William has a rich father."

9 **Albert and Antonie Mallet:** Albert and Antonie Mallet also traveled on the New York Express and were befriended by the Laroches. The Mallet family boarded the *Titanic* at Cherbourg-Octeville as second-class passengers and were heading to Montreal, where Albert worked as a cognac importer for Hormidas Laporte, the former Mayor of Montreal. Only Mrs. Mallet and her son, André, survived the sinking. After a brief return to her home in Montreal, Mrs. Mallet and André moved back to France, where they resided for the remainder of their lives. Mrs. Mallet died in 1974; André, in 1973.

10 **Hormidas Laporte:** Montreal businessman and financier who had served as Mayor of Montreal from 1904 to 1906. Albert Mallet had worked for Laporte's liquor importing firm for about seven or eight years until his death.

11 **André Mallet:** *See* Albert and Antonie Mallet.

12 **West Indies:** The Caribbean islands are sometimes referred to as the "West Indies." That's because, when Columbus stumbled upon some islands, he thought he'd reached the East Indies (Asia) on his voyage to find another route there. These islands were called the

"West Indies" to account for Columbus' mistake. His name for the inhabitants—"Indians"—is still often used.

13   **Rum:** The origin of the word *rum* is generally unclear. For quite some time people pointed to India as the land in which rum was first consumed and thus credited it with the word's creation. However, they did not realize that in other European languages *rum* was actually a borrowing from English. According to British etymologist Samuel Morewood, the word for the alcoholic beverage might have come from the British slang term for "the best," as in "having a rum time." In an 1824 essay about the word's origin, he wrote, "As spirits, extracted from molasses, could not well be ranked under the name whiskey, brandy, or arrack, it would be called *rum*, to denote its excellence or superior quality."

14   ***Nomadic:*** The passengers from the *New York Express* were transferred to the *Nomadic*, one of two ferries that transported first- and second-class passengers from the pier to the *Titanic*. The White Star Line (Oceanic Steam Navigation Company) needed to bring passengers and their baggage to and from the liners waiting off the port at Cherbourg-Octeville. Other shipping lines used converted passenger ferries, but White Star Line ordered new purpose-built tenders. *Nomadic* is preserved on Queen's Island, Belfast, and open to visitors.

15   **White Star Line:** White Star Line ticket number 2123 had a price tag of forty-one pounds. According to the website *Titanic Story*, "Many of the passengers were not originally supposed to be traveling on the *Titanic*. Due to a strike, coal was in short supply. This shortage threatened *Titanic's* maiden voyage and forced the White Star Line to cancel travel on the *Oceanic* and *Adriatic* and transfer their passengers and coal stocks to the *Titanic*."

16   ***Traffic:*** According to Titanic Belfast, *Traffic* transported "third-class passengers, cargo and baggage with an added feature—baggage creepers

[carousels]—similar to those used today by the airlines. Innovation was key not only to maintaining White Star Line's position as one of the world's greatest shipping lines but also established Harland & Wolff as a world-class shipbuilder."

17   **Charles Hays:** Charles Melville Hays (1856–1912) was president of the Grand Trunk Railway. He began as a clerk at the age of seventeen and worked his way up to become the vice president of the Wabash, St. Louis and Pacific Railway. He remained in this position until 1896, when he became general manager of the Grand Trunk Railway of Canada. He was a first-class passenger on the RMS *Titanic*. One hour before the disaster, Hays expressed concern that "the trend to playing fast and loose with larger and larger ships will end in tragedy." A few minutes later, *Titanic* struck the iceberg. Hays drowned in the sinking, though his wife and four daughters fortunately survived the tragedy.

18   **J. Bruce Ismay**: Joseph Bruce Ismay (1862–1937) served as chairman and managing director of the White Star Line. He came to international attention as the highest-ranking White Star official to survive the sinking of the *Titanic*. As a result, he was subject to severe criticism and derided by the press for boarding a lifeboat when there were still women and children aboard the vessel.

19   **Turkish baths:** On the *Titanic*, Turkish baths were exclusive first-class accommodations. They were designed in a Moorish style with heated blankets and service waiters. Ken Marshall, famous for his photorealistic renderings, has illustrated many parts of the *Titanic*, including the Turkish Baths. The Turkish baths are also featured in the computer game *Titanic: Adventure Out of Time*.

20   **Squash court:** Squash is a ball sport played by two (singles) or four players (doubles) in a four-walled court with a small, hollow rubber ball. The players must alternate in striking the ball with their racquet and hitting the ball onto the playable surfaces of the

four walls of the court. According to Sam Dangremond of *Town and Country Magazine*, the first players used rubber balls, which, when hit, squashed against walls (hence the name "squash"). The *Titanic* had a squash court and professional Fred Wright went down with the ship.

21 **Parisian Café:** The **Café Parisien** was a Parisian-style café on the RMS *Titanic*. On April 14th, the night *Titanic* struck an iceberg, the menu included oysters, salmon, roast duckling, beef sirloin, pâté de foie gras, peaches in Chartreuse jelly, and chocolate and vanilla éclairs.

22 **Captain Edward John Smith**: Edward John Smith (1850–1912) was the captain of the *Titanic* and perished when the ship sank. Smith left school early to join the British Merchant Navy and the Royal Naval Reserve. After earning his master's ticket, he entered the service of the White Star Line. His first command was the *SS Celtic*. He eventually served as commanding officer of numerous White Star Line vessels, including the *Majestic*, which he commanded for nine years. In 1904, Smith became the commodore of the White Star Line, and was responsible for controlling its flagships. He successfully commanded the *Baltic*, *Adriatic*, and the *Olympic*. Smith was posthumously lauded as an example of British stoicism for his conduct aboard the *Titanic*, and his refusal to evacuate as it sank.

23 **Queenstown:** Queenstown is a maritime town in Ireland, known as the *Titanic*'s last port of call. On April 11th, 1912, at 11:30 a.m., *Titanic* dropped the anchor in Queenstown. Tenders *Ireland* and *America* were waiting in the dock to transport 123 passengers out to board—sixty-three men and sixty women, for many of whom Queenstown was the gateway to a great new world. Of the 123 passengers that boarded in Queenstown, three were first class, seven were second class while the remaining 113 were third class (steerage). Just forty-four of the passengers that embarked from Queenstown survived.

24   **the music band:** "Many brave things were done that night but none more brave than by those few men playing minute after minute as the ship settled quietly lower and lower in the sea...the music they played serv[ed] alike as their own immortal requiem and their right to be recorded on the rules of undying fame." —Lawrence Beesley, *Titanic* Survivor

25   **Lifeboat no. 8**: During the sinking of the *Titanic*, Mrs. Laroche and her children climbed on Lifeboat no. 8 (although some sources point to Lifeboat no. 14). Joseph was left behind as only women and children were allowed to get on the lifeboats. Lifeboat no. 8 was the first portside lifeboat to be lowered and launched, at about 1:00 a.m. or 1:20 a.m., under the supervision of Second Officer Lightoller. The occupants of lifeboat no. 8 numbered approximately twenty-five people, including Noëlle, Countess of Rothes, who took charge of the lifeboat's tiller and helped row when it became apparent that the crewmen aboard were not oarsmen. When some suggested that the occupants aid those who were swimming in the ocean, only three aboard agreed. The others were worried swimmers desperate to escape death by drowning would capsize the boat. After spending the long night rowing toward what they believed were lights from a rescue ship on the horizon, the occupants of Lifeboat no. 8 had a long row back when the *Carpathia* arrived at dawn from the opposite direction they had headed. They were not picked up until 7:30 a.m. According to Olivier Mendes, from the Titanic Historical Society, "Neither Madame Mallet nor Laroche could remember what number lifeboat they had escaped. The only detail Juliette remembered was that in her boat a countess or someone with a title was among those who rowed all night long. The boat had icy water in the bottom and her feet were frozen."

"I saw the way she was carrying herself and the quiet, determined manner in which she spoke, and I knew she was more of a man than most aboard, so I put her in command at the tiller. There was another woman in the boat who helped,

and was every minute rowing. It was she who suggested we
should sing, and we sang as we rowed, starting with 'Pull for
the Shore.' We were still singing when we saw the lights of the
Carpathia, and then we stopped singing and prayed."
—Seaman Thomas Jones praised the courage of the Countess of
Rothes in lifeboat number eight

"And it wasn't until we were in the lifeboat and
rowing away, it wasn't until then [that] I realized that
ship's going to sink. It hits me there."
—Eva Hart, *Titanic* survivor

26   *Carpathia:* RMS *Carpathia* was a Cunard Line transatlantic
passenger steamship built by Swan Hunter & Wigham Richardson
in Newcastle upon Tyne, England. On her maiden voyage in 1903,
Carpathia traveled from Liverpool to Boston. In April 1912, *Carpathia*
became famous for her role in the rescue efforts following the sinking
of the *Titanic,* a dangerous rescue mission that involved traveling
through treacherous ice fields. *Carpathia* arrived within two hours of
the *Titanic*'s sinking and rescued 705 of its survivors from lifeboats.
On July 17, 1918, RMS *Carpathia* sank off the southern coast of
Ireland after being torpedoed by the German submarine SM U-55.

"Icebergs loomed up and fell astern and we never slackened.
It was an anxious time with the Titanic's fateful experience
very close in our minds. There were 700 souls on Carpathia
and those lives as well as the survivors of the Titanic herself
depended on the sudden turn of the wheel."
—Captain Arthur H. Rostron, Commander of Carpathia

27   **The Titanic Historical Society:** The Titanic Historical Society is
a nonprofit organization with the purpose of preserving the history
of the famous ocean liner. From their website: "The Society is the
authority and source for the *Titanic* and the White Star Line and for
four decades has maintained that goal. Its main field of endeavor

is *The Titanic Commutator*, the Society's official journal, insuring a permanent record of information."

28 **Edward Kamuda:** Edward Stephen Kamuda (1939-2014) was an American historian who specialized in the study of the RMS *Titanic*. Kamuda devoted much of his life to the preservation of the *Titanic's* legacy and was the founder and president of the Titanic Historical Society. His research primarily focused on the biographies of the crew and passengers of the *Titanic*. He, along with several other society members, served as a technical consultant on the 1997 James Cameron film *Titanic,* and was an extra in the film. He traveled from the United States to France to attend the Cherbourg-Octeville tribute.

29 **Michel Navratil Jr.:** At three-and-a-half years old, Michel Navratil Jr. (1908-2001) was on board the *Titanic* after he and his brother Edmond were kidnapped by their father. According to *Encyclopedia Titanica*, on the night of the sinking, when their father brought Michel and Edmond to the deck, Second Officer Charles Lightoller had ordered a locked-arms circle of crew members around Collapsible D (the last and ninth lifeboat lowered on the port side) so that only women and children could get through. Navratil Sr. handed the boys through the ring of men, and reportedly gave Michel Jr. a final message: "My child, when your mother comes for you, as she surely will, tell her that I loved her dearly and still do. Tell her I expected her to follow us, so that we might all live happily together in the peace and freedom of the New World." When the boys were rescued, the international media was enraptured by the mystery surrounding them. Finally, their mother, who lived in Nice, recognized them from the papers and embarked from Cherbourg-Octeville to bring them back home. Six years after the Cherbourg tribute, the Navratil boys and Louise Laroche met again in Paris with another survivor, an English nonagenarian named Millvina Dean.

30 *La Patrie: La Patrie,* a daily newspaper in Quebec, speculated that the Navatril children belonged to Joseph Laroche.

31   **Millvina Dean:** Eliza Gladys "Millvina" Dean (1912–2009) was a British civil servant, cartographer, and the last survivor of the sinking of the RMS *Titanic* on April 15, 1912. At two months old, she was also the youngest passenger aboard. In an interview with *The New York Times*, Ms. Dean said all she knew of what happened during the sinking she had learned from her mother: "She told me that they heard a tremendous crash, and that my father went up on deck, then came back down again and said, 'Get the children up and take them to the deck as soon as possible, because the ship has struck an iceberg.'"

32   **Cap-Haïtien:** A port city in the mountainous north coast region of Haiti. It was founded in 1670 by the French and was originally known as Cap-Français. It gained early renown as the "Paris of the Antilles" for its stunning architecture and cultural offerings. It served as capital of Saint-Domingue until 1770 and was the scene of slave uprisings in 1791. The city was razed by French and Haitian troops in 1802 but was later rebuilt under the reign of King Henri Christophe. After the revolution (around 1820), he proclaimed it the capital of the Northern Kingdom of Haiti. Cap-Haïtien was Haiti's most important city for a long time until Port-au-Prince relegated it to second place. Joseph Laroche was born in Cap-Haïtien, which is often referred as Le Cap or Okap.

33   **Euzélie Laroche:** Anne Euzélie Laroche, known as Zélie, (1862–1952) was the mother of Joseph Laroche, who carried her family name. She was born in the municipality of Grande Rivière du Nord, 160 kilometers (about ninety-nine miles) from Cap-Haïtien. Mrs. Laroche specialized in trade and built a fortune through her Kay-Café.

34   **Coffee:** Coffee was Haiti's main asset at the time and was sold through a network of Haitian business women called *madan sara*. Coffee production in Haiti has been important to its economy since the early eighteenth century, when the French brought the coffee plant to the colony then known as Saint-Domingue. It has been a principal

crop of Haiti ever since. At the present-day, coffee has fallen behind both mango and cocoa in terms of export value.

35   **Christina Schutt:** Christina Schutt (1973–) is a Haitian jurist whose great-grandfather was related to Euzélie Laroche.

36   **Madan sara speculators:** In Haiti, madan sara speculators are savvy businesswomen women who travel around the country to buy, distribute, and sell a variety of goods in different markets. Caroline Shenaz Hossein, an assistant professor in the Department of Social Science at York University (Toronto, Canada) points out that "in Haiti, madan saras have for centuries personalized economics through a *sistèm pratik* that has institutionalized market operations by connecting buyers and sellers." According to *The Haitian Observer*, "The Madan Sara creates an integral trading network, operating as a liaison between the more than 700,000 small farms in the rural and coastal areas and the buyers of produce within the city. She establishes a regular route for her travels, and maintains relationships with her contacts, making trading easier and bilateral, as often, buyers can also have something to sell and sellers want something to buy."

37   **Grande-Rivière du Nord:** Euzélie Laroche was born in the municipality of Grande Rivière du Nord, 160 kilometers from Cap-Haïtien. Grande-Rivière-du-Nord is a commune in the Grande-Rivière-du-Nord Arrondissement, in the Nord Department of Haiti. It is also the birthplace of Jean-Jacques Dessalines, one of Haiti's founding fathers, and the birthplace of Haiti's intelligentsia Jean Price Mars, who pioneered the Négritude movement, inspiring the "Black is Beautiful" slogan of the 1960s.

38   **Peter Gottlieb:** Peter Gottlieb was a German sailor dreaming of adventure who landed in Le Cap in 1841. Germans were welcome in Haiti and it seemed to him the ideal place to start a new life.

39   **Earthquake:** The island of Hispaniola is prone to tectonic shifts and earthquakes due to its location at the crux of several plate

boundaries between the North American Plate and the Caribbean Plate. The May 7, 1842 earthquake in Cap-Haïtien occurred at 5:00 p.m. local time. It had an estimated magnitude of 8.1 and triggered a destructive tsunami. The northern coast of Haiti and part of what is now the Dominican Republic experienced the greatest damage from the earthquake, but it was felt across the Antilles, in southern Cuba, Jamaica, and in Puerto Rico. Approximately 5,000 people were killed by the aftereffects of the earthquake and another 300 by the tsunami.

40   **Henri Laroche:** A cobbler in Haiti, Henri Laroche was a womanizer. By the time of his death, he would father between twenty-eight and thirty children, among them Euzélie Laroche. Henri lost two children in the earthquake. He eventually acknowledged all of his children.

41   **Cockfights:** Cockfighting is an ancient spectator sport that can be traced back at least 6,000 years. It was popular in Persia, India, and China, and spread northward into Europe after being introduced to Greece between 524-460, BC. Eventually, colonization and the transatlantic slave trade introduced it to the Western hemisphere. Cockfighting plays a central role in Alex Haley's novel *Roots*. In cockfights, specially bred gamecocks are equipped with metal spurs or knives, which are fastened over their natural leg spurs, and are released into a circular ring where they spar off against other gamecocks, often until one of the birds dies from their injuries. Cockfighting is illegal in most of the modern world but is still a popular pastime for many spectators who place bets on the outcome of the fighting matches. As a youngster in Haiti, Joseph often attended cockfights in open air arenas.

42   **Krik? Krak!:** Also "Tim Tim" in Haitian Creole, Krik? Krak! is the exchange that precedes a story. Krik? is the equivalent of "Would you like to hear a story?" The response, "Krak!" is the equivalent of "Yes!" Story telling was a part of Joseph Laroche's life in Haiti. As a

child, he enjoyed the tales of Bouki and Malice, and crafty animals like Anansi and Brother Rabbit taught Joseph life lessons.

43 **Bouki & Malice**: The stories of Bouki and Malice are some of the most famous trickster tales in Haitian folklore. In the tales, Ti Malice is the wily trickster and Uncle Bouki or Tonton Bouqui is hardworking, but greedy, and usually easy to trick because his greed gets the best of him. Bouki & Malice tales are thought to have originated in Senegal.

44 **Anansi**: Known as the King of Stories, Anansi is one of the most important characters in West African and Caribbean folklore. Often depicted as a spider, Anansi is a trickster figure who can change his appearance to look like a human or a variety of animal figures when it suits his need. He originated with the Ashanti people of Ghana, but his popularity spread throughout Africa and to the Caribbean.

45 **Brother Rabbit**: In the United States, Brother Rabbit is best known from the stories of Uncle Remus and Brer Rabbit. It is believed that Brother Rabbit originated in Senegal as the trickster figure Ti Malice and came to the Western hemisphere with the transatlantic slave trade, where he became popular throughout the Caribbean and American south, but scholars attribute the origin of the character to many different cultures with rabbit trickster figures, including Algonquin and Cherokee Indians. The famous Disney Film, *Song of the South*, features Brer Rabbit. A similar trickster figure is the character of Bugs Bunny in the Warner Brothers cartoons, who is thought to be based on Brother Rabbit.

46 **(The) Ville de Saint-Nazaire**: The *Ville de Saint-Nazaire*, full of merchandise for the West Indies, was en route from New York and scheduled to arrive in Le Cap on March 6, 1897. It never did. It went down due to a leak worsened by a hurricane off Cape Hatteras. Of the eighty-three passengers and crew on board, only eighteen survived.

47   **Marcel Héber-Suffrin:** Marcel Héber-Suffrin (1816–1914), a sailor from Martinique, was one of the eight survivors rescued in extremis from *Ville de Saint-Nazaire* by a passing ship.

48   **Salted Water:** While sodium chloride (salt) is a necessary part of the human diet, seawater is generally considered unsafe for human consumption. It can actually even lead to hypernatremia, which is an abnormally high concentration of sodium in the blood. Symptoms of hypernatremia include: weakness, nausea, loss of appetite, excessive thirst, confusion, muscle-twitching, and in more severe cases, brain swelling, which can lead to death as the brain presses against the interior cranial wall. The frustration of sailors who are without adequate supply of freshwater and are tempted to slake their thirst with seawater is most notably captured in the lines of Samuel Taylor Coleridge's "The Rime of the Ancient Mariner " (1798): "Water, water, everywhere,/And all the boards did shrink;/ Water, water, everywhere,/ Nor any drop to drink."

49   ***Franconia / Olinde Rodrigues:*** The RMS *Franconia* was one of the star ships of the time that sailed from Hamburg to the West Indies. Its name was later changed to *Olinde Rodrigues.*

50   **Émile Zola:** Literary master Émile Zola (1840–1902), who spearheaded the development of theatrical naturalism, failed his *baccalauréat* examination not once, but twice! That goes to show you: Even if you may not be a good student, you can still be successful in literature... or in life. Many famous authors of the nineteenth century lived on almost nothing, as their works were not recognized when they were alive. Zola actually made quite a bite of money as a writer during his lifetime.

51   **Loti:** Pierre Loti was the pseudonym of Louis Marie-Julien Viaud (1850–1923). He was a French naval officer and novelist, known for his exotic novels and short stories.

52   **Bourget:** Paul Charles Joseph Bourget (1852–1935) was a French novelist and critic. He was nominated for the Nobel Prize in Literature five times.

53   **(The)** *Santa Maria*: The *Santa Maria* was one of Christopher Columbus' caravels. It sank off the coast of Le Cap. According to Jonny Wikes, a contributor to the website *History Revealed*, "it is widely believed that the crews of the *Santa Maria*, *Nina*, and *Pinta* were mostly made up of criminals. Although it is true that a royal decree in Spain offered amnesty to any criminals who joined the voyage, only four men were actually convicts."

54   **(The)** *Saint Guillaume*: The *Saint Guillaume* was the last known sinking ship coming back from Guinea with 600 slaves on board. According to Duke University's website, the ship, archived as Vessel Identification Number (VIN) 24722 in the Slave Voyages database, "originated in Nantes, France; purchased slaves in Malembo, West Central Africa; and arrived in Saint-Domingue on August 27, 1775. According to the manifest, 250 Africans embarked but only 209 survived to disembark in the colony. Dramatically, the *Saint Guillaume* was shipwrecked and nearly lost off the coast of the Ile de la Gonave. However, it was reported 'the Crew and most of the Slaves saved.' " The ship hit a reef after a navigational error and was submerged by raging waters. The number on board is still disputed.

55   **Bertrand Laroche:** Bertrand Laroche was Euzélie Laroche's brother. He committed suicide on August 4, 1897 at the age of thirty-two.

56   **Arnold Laroche:** Arnold Laroche was Euzélie Laroche's nephew. He was a poet who killed himself in Paris. He wrote the famous poem "Les Plaintes de Toussaint Louverture au Fort de Joux." Toussaint's final prison was at Fort de Joux, in the Jura Mountains, not far from Switzerland. He arrived there in August of 1802, and the Minster of the Marine, following Bonaparte's orders, ensured that Toussaint's

conditions of imprisonment would be as difficult as possible. He died there on April 7, 1803.

57   **Dr. Nemours Auguste:** Dr. Nemours Auguste (1850–?) was the half-brother of Joseph Laroche's father and was married to Euzélie's niece. He was a notable Haitian diplomat and was chargé d'affaires to Jacques Nicolas Léger, Haiti's Secretary of State in 1912. His son was Alfred Auguste Nemours, a notable Haitian diplomat, military general and historian. He was an elegant and erudite physician who was also an astute businessman. Backed by French investors, Dr. Nemours Auguste proposed a railway project that was well received by the government.

58   **François Beaufaussé Laroche:** François Beaufaussé Laroche was Euzélie's nephew. He was a general in the military and minister of defense.

59   **Michel Oreste:** Michel Oreste Lafontant (1859–1918) served as president of Haiti from May 1913 to January 1914. He won the presidential elections in Haiti over François Beaufaussé Laroche, Euzélie's nephew, a general in the military and minister of defense. Michel Oreste was a reformist toppled by forces loyal to landowner elites such as his successor Oreste Zamor. He died in exile in New York City in 1918.

60   **Raoul Auguste:** Raoul Auguste (1855–1908) was once romantically involved with Euzélie Laroche. He was Joseph Laroche's father and the cousin of Haitian president Tancrède Auguste.

61   **Louis Price-Mars:** Louis Price-Mars (1906–2000) was a notorious Haitian psychiatrist.

62   **Anténor Firmin:** Joseph Auguste Anténor Firmin (1850–1911), also known as Anténor Firmin, was a Haitian anthropologist, journalist, and politician, best known for his book *De l'égalité des races humaines* (*On the Equality of Human Races*, 1885), which argued that "all men

are endowed with the same qualities and the same faults, without distinction of color or anatomical form. The races are equal" (pp. 450). The book was published as a rebuttal to French writer Count Arthur de Gobineau's work *Essay on the Inequality of Human Races*.

63   **Cincinnatus Leconte:** Jean-Jacques Dessalines Michel Cincinnatus Leconte (1854–1912) was President of Haiti from August 15, 1911 until his death on August 8, 1912. He was the great-grandson of Jean-Jacques Dessalines—a leader of the Haitian Revolution and the first ruler of an independent Haiti. Joseph Laroche was Leconte's nephew. A lawyer by trade, Leconte was forced into exile after a 1908 coup deposed of President Pierre Nord Alexis, the Haitian president under whom Leconte served as minister of the interior. Leconte led a successful rebellion from exile in 1911 and was unanimously elected President of Haiti by Congress on August 14, 1911. Leconte was killed in a mysterious explosion at the presidential palace in Port-au-Prince in August of 1912, just months after his nephew perished in the sinking of the *Titanic*.

64   **Tancrède Auguste:** Tancrède Auguste (1856–1913) was Joseph Laroche's paternal uncle. Following Cincinnatus Leconte's death, Auguste became Haiti's twentieth president in August 1912. The president died within less than two years in office, and many believed that he was poisoned. Following the death of Tancrède Auguste, Haiti witnessed the arrival and departure of five presidents, among them the first civilian president Michel Oreste, elected on May 4, 1913.

65   **Emile Lüders:** In September of 1897, Emile Lüders, a German citizen (1842–1911), born in Haiti to a German father and a Haitian mother, was arrested for assaulting a policeman outside the Central Stables in Port-au-Prince, where he was the proprietor. Lüders had previously served a sentence for assaulting a policeman in Haiti. After serving a second prison sentence for the 1897 assault, Lüders was deported to Germany and fined for the assault. In response to his arrest and deportation, Germany sent two armed warships to the harbor outside

of Port-au-Prince, presented a list of demands including restitution and repatriation to Haiti for Lüders, and threatened to bombard the city if the Haitian government did not acquiesce to their demands in what became known as the Lüders Affair.

66   **(The) Lüders Affair:** The Lüders Affair was a legal and diplomatic embarrassment to the Haitian government. In September of 1897, Emile Lüders, a German citizen, born in Haiti to a German father and a Haitian mother, was arrested for assaulting a policeman outside the Central Stables in Port-au-Prince, where he was the proprietor. Following the arrest, Count von Schwerin, the German chargé d'affaires in 1897, reported the mistreatment of a German national to his government and requested military support. On December 6, 1897, two German warships, SMS *Charlotte* and SMS *Stein*, dropped anchor outside Port-au-Prince. A written ultimatum delivered to President Sam demanded $20,000 in compensation be given to Lüders for false arrest, his safe passage back to Haiti, a formal apology to the German government, a twenty-one-gun salute to the German flag and a reception to honor Schwerin. Sam was given four hours to agree or face open fire from the warships docked in the harbor. Sam raised the white flag in surrender, but ultimately lost the presidency in the aftermath of the incident.

67   **Count Schwerin:** Count von Schwerin was the German chargé d'affaires during the Lüders Affair of 1897. He was tasked with overseeing a community of about two hundred Germans, mostly coffee traders, in Haiti. After the arrest of Emile Lüders, a German citizen, Schwerin demanded Lüders' immediate release as well as the firing of the police officers involved. When the US minister Powell also insisted that Lüders should be set free, the issue swiftly reached the desk of President Tirésias Simon Sam. For perhaps understandable reasons, Sam duly gave in, and Lüders left Haiti for Hamburg.

68   **Tirésias Simon Sam:** Tirésias Antoine Augustin Simon Sam (1835–1916), a popular general in Haiti's confused and overstaffed

army, rose to become the country's president in the year 1896, one week after his predecessor, Florvil Hippolyte, suffered a fatal stroke while en route to stamp out a revolt in the Southwest. Nicknamed "The Incompetent," Sam ushered in the twentieth century at the head of a cynically corrupt and increasingly unpopular administration. He resigned before the completion of his six-year presidential term.

69 **German warships:**

SMS *Charlotte* was a German steam corvette launched in September 1885 and commissioned in November 1886. The only vessel of her class, *Charlotte* was the last sailing warship built for the German navy. She was armed with a battery of eighteen 15-cm (5.9-in) guns. The ship remained in service until May 1909.

SMS *Stein* was a Bismarck-class corvette built for the German Imperial Navy in the late 1870s. She was named after the Prussian statesman Heinrich Friedrich Karl vom und zum Stein. *Stein* launched in September 1879 and was commissioned into the fleet in October 1880. She was armed with a battery of twelve 15-cm (5.9-in) guns and had a full ship rig to supplement her steam engine on long cruises abroad.

70 **Captain Karl Batsch:** According to historian Jacques Nicholas Léger, author of *Haiti, Her History, and Her Detractors*, the Haitians openly showed their sympathy for France during the Franco-Prussian war, which displeased Germany. After Germany prevailed in the war, Captain Karl Ferdinand Batsch seized two Haitian naval ships, demanding the payment of £3,000. Indignant at this attack, the Haitian people—in the words of poet Oswald Durand—"threw the money to the Germans as one would cast a bone to a dog." The ships were eventually returned with the Haitian flag stained with excrement, and Germany's actions caused long-lived resentment.

71 **Oswald Durand:** Oswald Durand (1840–1906) was a Haitian politician, but also a writer and poet of French and Creole

expression, considered the national poet of Haiti. He was "to Haiti what Shakespeare is to England and Dante to Italy." His most famous works are *Choucoune*, a lyrical poem praising the beauty of a Haitian woman, and *Chant National*, a lyrical historic poem which became as popular as the presidential hymn.

72 **Ayiti**: *Ayiti* is the Haitian Creole word for Haiti. It comes from both Native American and African terms. It means "land of high mountains" in the Taino-Arawak Native American language, and "sacred earth or homeland" in the Fon African language.

73 **Arawaks**: The Arawak are a group of indigenous peoples who populated South America and the Greater Antilles. One of their subgroups, the Taino, were the first tribe to have contact with Christopher Columbus on his arrival to the island of Hispaniola. The Taino were effectively destroyed when their lack of immunity meant they easily succumbed to the illnesses Spaniards inadvertently brought over.

74 **Vincent Ogé**: (1775–1791) and Jean-Baptiste Chavannes (1748–1791) were rebels who protested the oppression of people of color by the French colonial authorities. After they were captured, they were brutally tortured and executed on February 21, 1791 in Le Cap in the presence of the provincial assembly and authorities.

75 **Jean-Baptiste Chavannes**: Jean-Baptiste Chavannes (1748–1791) was a Haitian abolitionist and soldier. In 1778, he volunteered to assist the US Continental Army. He distinguished himself during the American Revolutions in operations in Virginia, New York, and the retreat from Savannah in December 1778. Once the war was over and independence declared, Chavannes returned to Haiti. During a revolt in 1790 near Cap-Français, Chavannes (who supported total abolition of slavery) fled to safety on the Spanish side of the island. The Haitian requested his extradition, according to treaty. He was delivered to Haitian authorities on December 21,1790 and sentenced to execution by hammering.

76   **Toussaint Louverture:** Toussaint Louverture (1743–1803), born
      in slavery as the son of the African prince Gaou Guinon, was Haiti's
      greatest warrior and one of its founding fathers. Born on a plantation
      near le Cap, Toussaint Louverture was the first black general in the
      French army, the first black governor of a colony, the first leader of a
      slave-led revolution, the father of the independent Republic, and the
      "governor for life" of Haiti. Louverture freed the slaves of Haiti—in
      the only permanently successful slave revolt in history—and wrote
      the first constitution for Haiti. After paving the way for others to win
      the fight for freedom, Toussaint died in prison only six months before
      Haitian Independence Day. In Joseph Laroche's family, Toussaint
      Louverture was venerated because he embodied the Haitian fight
      for freedom.

He died in French captivity in the dungeon at Fort de Joux on April
7, 1803. The sonnet "To Toussaint L'Ouverture" by the British poet
William Wordsworth shows how closely Toussaint Louverture's
actions—and, later, his imprisonment—were followed around the world.

O TOUSSAINT L'OUVERTURE
TOUSSAINT, the most unhappy of men!
Whether the whistling Rustic tend his plough
Within thy hearing, or thy head be now
Pillowed in some deep dungeon's earless den;
O miserable Chieftain! where and when
Wilt thou find patience? Yet die not; do thou
Wear rather in thy bonds a cheerful brow:
Though fallen thyself, never to rise again,
Live, and take comfort. Thou hast left behind
Powers that will work for thee; air, earth, and skies;
There's not a breathing of the common wind
That will forget thee; thou hast great allies;
Thy friends are exultations, agonies,
And love, and man's unconquerable mind.

77 **Fort-de-Joux:** Located in the Jura mountains, near Switzerland, Fort-de-Joux was built in the twelfth century. Between 1678 and 1815, it became a state prison for domestic and foreign prisoners, including Toussaint Louverture, leader of Saint-Domingue's slave insurrection.

78 **La Dessalinienne:** *La Dessalinienne* is the Haitian national anthem. It bears the name of the father of independence, Jean-Jacques Dessalines. According to Dr. Rebecca Dirksen in her article, "Haiti's Centennial and the Dessalinienne," the anthem was officially introduced to the public on January 1st, 1904, "as crowds numbering in the thousands were guided through singing the words and melody during the Independence Day celebration. [...] An additional historical moment involving this piece of music occurred when the Haitian national army band played *La Dessalinienne* on the final day of the US Occupation (1915–1934) in recognition of Haiti's re-established sovereignty. Significantly, the national anthem was not translated from French into Haitian Kreyòl, the language of the majority of the population, until the popular vocalist Ansy Dérose began performing a Kreyòl version in 1986."

79 **Alexandre Pétion:** In 1807, Alexandre Sabès Pétion (1770–1818) became the first president of the Republic of Haiti. He is one of Haiti's founding fathers, along with Toussaint Louverture, Jean-Jacques Dessalines, and Henri Christophe. The Port-au-Prince suburb Pétion-Ville is named in his honor. He was biracial, born in Haiti to a Haitian mulatto mother and a wealthy French father (who withheld his name because the child was too dark). The name Pétion came from the French-patois nickname Pichon, which means "my little one."

80 **Henri Christophe:** Henri Christophe (1767–1820) was the sole monarch of the Kingdom of Haiti. Christophe was a former slave who rose to power in the ranks of the Haitian revolutionary military. After Dessalines was assassinated, Christophe created a separate government in the north of Haiti. He is known for constructing

Citadel Henri (now known as Citadelle Laferrière), the Sans-Souci Palace, and numerous other palaces and fortresses, in the hopes it would make French incursion in the event of an attack less likely. In August of 1820, King Christophe suffered a stroke and became paralyzed. When his army abandoned him, he killed himself with a self-inflicted gunshot on October 8, 1820.

81 **Jean-Pierre Boyer:** Jean-Pierre Boyer (1776–1850) was one of the leaders in the Haitian Revolution. He served as president of Haiti from 1818 to 1843. Jean-Pierre Boyer reunified the entire country after the death of King Christophe in 1820 and annexed Spanish Haiti, which brought all of Hispaniola under one Haitian government rule. Boyer's demands and reforms in Spanish Haiti created high levels of resentment, and on February 27, 1844, the Trinitarios (a secret society of young Dominican rebels) marched on the Puerta del Conde in Santo Domingo, and declared Dominican independence from Haiti. When present-day Dominicans celebrate their national independence on this date, they are marking their separation not from the Spanish Crown, but from their neighbors to the west of the island.

82 **Aimé Césaire**: Aimé-Fernand-David Césaire (1913–2008) was a poet, playwright, and politician. Born in St. Martin, Césaire was educated in Paris, and along with Léopold Sédar Senghor, co-founded "Négritude," an influential movement to restore the cultural identity of black Africans, which he later abandoned in favor of black militancy. He dedicated a theatrical piece to King Christophe, a key leader in the Haitian Revolution.

83 **Sans-Souci palace:** According to Canadian historian Gauvin Alexander Bailey, "Sans-Souci palace was the royal residence of King Henri I (better known as Henri Christophe) of Haiti, Queen Marie-Louise and their two daughters. It was the most important of nine palaces built by the king, as well as fifteen châteaux, numerous forts, and sprawling summer homes on his twenty plantations. Construction

of the palace started in 1810 and was completed in 1813. Its name translated from French means 'carefree.' "

84   **Luc Grimard:** Luc Grimard (1886–1954) was a Haitian writer, educator, and diplomat.

85   **Haiti and the Vatican:** Haiti signed a concordat with the Vatican in March 1860 to normalize its relations with the church. Prior to this concordat, the Vatican had withdrawn its priests in 1804 and refused to acknowledge Haiti's sovereignty after Haiti declared independence. This concordat allowed Haiti to communicate directly with the Vatican and to set up a diocese system. It also helped Haiti come out of diplomatic isolation.

86   **St. Joseph de Cluny:** The Sisters of St. Joseph of Cluny is a Roman Catholic religious institute founded in 1807. With locations found around the world, its members perform a variety of charitable works, but they devote themselves especially to missionary work and providing education for the poor. In 1872, the nuns of St. Joseph de Cluny founded a religious school for girls in Le Cap.

87   **Brothers of Christian Instruction**: The Brothers of Christian Instruction, more commonly known as the La Mennais Brothers, is a Catholic educational organization that originated in France in 1819. Their aim remains that of their founders, Gabriel Deshayes and Jean-Marie de la Mennais: "to educate the young and to make Jesus Christ better known and better loved." The brothers are bound by the simple vows of poverty, chastity, and obedience. The organization dedicated itself to promoting education among the working class in France and, eventually, across the world. In 1878, the Brothers of Christian Instruction opened a school for boys. It was attended by Joseph Laroche.

88   **Lycée National du Cap:** Lycée National du Cap was a renowned non-denominational school with a Haitian principal.

89 **His Grace Kersuzan:** His Grace Kersuzan was Le Cap's bishop. He later took over Sainte Marie, a school created by Edmond Etienn (a brilliant and successful teacher who served as a role model for students). His Grace Kesruzan launched an anti-superstition campaign with the ambition to fight Vodou; he believed that the infusion of the morality of the gospel would enhance the lives of Haitians. His Grace Kersuzan was also opposed to the Protestants because they embodied the American model rejected by France and missionaries.

90 **Vodou:** Vodou is a religion practiced in Haiti. His Grace Kersuzan launched an anti-superstition campaign with the ambition to fight Vodou. This campaign was premised on the idea that eradicating Voudou and teaching the gospel's ethical framework would increase Haitians' quality of life. In her book, *The Spirits and the Law: Vodou and Power in Haiti,* Kate Ramsey writes that, "Kersuzan charged that those who practiced [Vodou] were not simply superstitious, but idolatrous, in endowing 'saints, images, [and] relics with exaggerated or ridiculous attributes.'" She explains that "Kersuzan appealed [...] to elite Haitian patriotism in emphasizing the high stakes of establishing national honor: 'It is a question of rehabilitating ourselves in the eyes of the civilized world, it is a question of saving our very existence gravely compromised by the vampires who suck our fortune.' The end of [Vodou] would prove to the world that an African-descended people could indeed 'civilize themselves, govern themselves, and, finally, form a nation worthy of this name.'"

91 **Protestants:** Protestants in Haiti are a significant minority of the population. The CIA Factbook reports that around 28.5 percent of the population is Protestant (Baptist 15.4 percent, Pentecostal 7.9 percent, Adventist 3 percent, Methodist 1.5 percent, other 0.7 percent). According to the US Library of Congress, "For many Haitians, Protestantism represented an opposition to Vodou. When people converted to Protestantism, they usually did not reject Vodou, but they often came to view the folk religion as diabolical. Most

Protestant denominations considered all *loas*, including family spirits, as demons. Some Haitians converted to Protestantism when they wanted to reject family spirits that they felt had failed to protect them. Others chose to become Protestants merely as a way to gain an alternative form of protection from misfortune."

92   **Giuseppe Verdi:** Giuseppe Fortunino Francesco Verdi (1813–1901) was an Italian opera composer. He was born near Busseto to a family of moderate means and received a musical education with assistance from a local patron. By his thirties, he had become one of the pre-eminent opera composers in history. He also briefly served as an elected politician.

93   **Toulouse-Lautrec:** According to blogger Cassie Fairy, "Toulouse-Lautrec was not only a French artist in the post-impressionist period, he was quite a character too! [...] He loved a good party and was renowned for turning up at events in a fancy dress. [...] As a big fan of absinthe, Toulouse-Lautrec decided to develop his own recipe for a cocktail containing the spirit. The drink was named 'Tremblement de Terre' or 'The Earthquake' because it was a strong mixture with cognac." He lived from 1864 to 1901.

94   **William McKinley:** William McKinley (1843–1901) was the twenty-fifth president of the United States. According to the magazine *Mental Floss*, during a public reception on Sept. 6, 1901 at the Pan-American Exposition in Buffalo, NY, Leon Czolgosz shot McKinley twice in the torso while the president greeted guests in a receiving line. "McKinley allegedly uttered, 'Don't let them hurt him,' as the angry mob descended on Czolgosz. Later, at the Emergency Hospital on the Exposition grounds, McKinley said of his assassin, 'It must have been some poor misguided fellow,' and 'He didn't know, poor fellow, what he was doing. He couldn't have known.' "

95 **Ministry in Haiti:** Maintaining religious ministries in Haiti was not easy due to various diseases and the lack of infrastructure. The only means to spread the gospel to farmers was by horseback.

96 **Beauvais:** Beauvais is a city and commune in northern France. Joseph Laroche attended the Institut Agricole de Beauvais to begin training as an agronomic engineer. According to the French Moments website, one of the city's landmarks, the Beauvais Cathedral (which has been described as "ambitious and gravity-defying") boasts the record for the highest ceiling in a gothic choir. In fact, it was the tallest monument in the Christendom for four consecutive years until its lantern tower tragically collapsed.

97 **Institution du St. Esprit:** According to their website, Institution du St. Esprit in Beauvais, France is a private Catholic boarding school that prepares children for superior education. The school was opened in 1889 by the St. Esprit Fathers. After the school was destroyed during the Second World War, a new establishment with the same name was built.

98 **Défilé the Madwoman:** Marie Sainte Dédée Bazile (?–about 1816) is considered one of four symbolic heroines of the fight for Haitian independence, alongside Sanité Bélair, Catherine Flon, and Cécile Fatiman. Born to enslaved parents near Cap-Français, the cause of Bazile's mental illness is disputed. Some claim it developed as the result of a rape by her master at the age of eighteen; some claim it developed after members of her family died in the Haitian revolution. A devoted follower of Emperor Dessalines, Bazile earned her living by selling provisions to his troops. She is known for having recovered Dessalines' remains and transporting them to the cemetery for a proper burial. She died about 1816. Her own gravesite location is unknown.

99   **Jean-Baptiste Déjoie Laroche:** Jean-Baptiste Déjoie Laroche was a physician living in Paris. He launched himself into politics and ran for president of Haiti without success. He was Joseph Laroche's uncle.

100   **Dodgeball:** The origins of dodgeball are disputed, with some scholars placing the origin of the sport at about 500 BC in Mesoamerica, Greece, or Asia. It was first observed by a missionary in Africa, Dr. James H. Carville. In its African form, the sport was a method of training warriors and was played with rocks instead of a rubber ball. The aim was to injure or kill the opposing team members to both foster teamwork, and to weed out weakness and develop agility. Dr. Carville brought a variation of the sport back with him to Norfolk, England, where it was played at St. Mary's College, using a much safer, but still painful leather ball. It came to the United States in 1884 when Phillip Ferguson returned to Yale from a trip to St. Mary's College, where he observed the sport. By 1905, he had redesigned the game and established the modern set of rules.

101   **Spinning top:** A spinning top is a toy designed to spin rapidly on the ground, the motion of which causes it to remain precisely balanced on its tip due to its rotational inertia. According to the *Art of Play* website, "Spin tops are among the oldest toys ever discovered by archaeologists. A clay top unearthed in Iraq was dated to thirty-fifth century BC—nearly six thousand years ago." Spinning top was played by the students in both Institution du St. Esprit and St. Joseph the Cluny.

102   **Hopscotch:** Hopscotch is a popular playground game in which players toss a small object into a pattern of numbered triangles or rectangles outlined on the ground and then hop or jump through the spaces to retrieve the object. Some scholars attest that Roman children played an ancient variation of the game, but the first written references to the game date to the late seventeenth century. In the English-speaking world the game was referred to as "scotch-hop" or

"scotch-hopper(s)." Hopscotch was played by the students in both Institution du St. Esprit and St. Joseph the Cluny.

103 **Skipped rope:** A "skipping rope" (British English) or "jump rope" (American English) is a tool used in the sport of skipping/ jump rope where one or more participants jump over a rope swung so that it passes under their feet and over their heads. Skipped rope was played by the students in both Institution du St. Esprit and St. Joseph the Cluny.

104 **Father Charles Beauvais:** Father Charles Beauvais was a St. Esprit alumnus who became a teacher of natural science, physics and history at the school.

105 **Francs:** The franc (F) is the name for the currency used in several different countries. The French franc was the currency of France until the euro was adopted in 1999.

106 **(The) Dreyfus Affair:** The Dreyfus Affair was a political scandal that erupted in France in 1896 and saw its resolution in 1904. It has become a notable example of a miscarriage of justice and exposed antisemitism within the French political system and army. The scandal began when in December 1894 Captain Alfred Dreyfus, a young Alsatian French artillery officer of Jewish descent, was sentenced to life imprisonment on Devil's Island for allegedly providing the German Embassy in Paris with French military secrets. After five years on Devil's Island, Captain Dreyfus was retried and found guilty in 1899. He was ultimately exonerated and released in 1906 when police discovered that another French officer was the real culprit. Dreyfus returned to the French Army and served the entirety of World War I, eventually being promoted to Lieutenant Colonel. Dreyfus died in 1935.

107 **Devil's Island:** The French penal colony of Cayenne, more commonly known as Devil's Island, was a notorious prison colony in the Salvation's Islands of French Guiana that operated between 1852

and 1953. Completely surrounded by water, the prison was nearly impossible to escape, and was known for its lack of sanitation and the cruelty of the prison guards. At its worst, the prison reported a seventy-five percent death rate before it was finally shut down in 1953. It was the destination of choice for French political dissidents of the period. Alfred Dreyfus was deported to Devil's Island.

108   **Jews in Haiti**: The first Jew to arrive in Haiti landed in 1492 was Luis de Torres, an interpreter for Christopher Columbus. During French colonization in 1633, many Dutch Jews arrived from Brazil in 1634 to work the French sugar plantations. In 1683, the Code Noir (Black Code), which forbade religions other than Roman Catholicism, led to the expulsion of Jews from all French colonies. Having seen promising changes, many returned in the mid-1700s , but were then either murdered or expelled during the slave revolt led by Toussaint Louverture. Later, missionaries in Haiti adopted shocking discriminatory attitudes toward the Jews because of the Dreyfus Affair, which involved a Jewish artillery captain in the French army, Alfred Dreyfus, who was falsely convicted of passing military secrets to the Germans.

109   **Félix Faure:** Félix François Faure (1841–1899) was the president of France from 1895 until his death in 1899. He is notable for his participation in the Dreyfus Affair, an involvement pro-Dreyfus intellectuals and politicians greatly criticized.

110   **Emile Loubet**: Émile François Loubet (1838–1929) was the 45th Prime Minister of France and later became President of France. During his tenure as president (1899–1906), Loubet saw the successful Paris Exhibition of 1900. Under his administration, the French Chamber of Deputies adopted the total separation of church and state. He pardoned Dreyfus and ended the Dreyfus affair after years of scandal and legal complications.

111   **Waldeck-Rousseau:** Pierre Waldeck-Rousseau was a French Republican politician who served as Prime Minister of France. He obtained a presidential pardon for Alfred Dreyfus.

112   **Law of Associations:** The Law of Associations (1901) suppressed nearly all of the religious orders in France and confiscated their property. The separation law (1905) sundered church and state, effectively overturing the Law of Associations.

113   **(The) *Novateur*:** *Le Novateur* was a newspaper in Le Cap.

114   **Labadee (French: Labadie):** Labadee is a port city on the northern coast of Haiti with spectacular beaches.

115   **Clugny market:** Clugny market is the main marketplace of Le Cap. Today, the market's stalls sell everything from live chickens and raw fish to bags of rice and secondhand clothing.

116   **Pumpkin soup:** Pumpkin soup is a traditional soup made out of squash that Haitians enjoy on New Year's Day, which is also Haitian Independence Day. According to the magazine *Epicurious*, "Haitian slaves were not allowed to have this delicious and aromatic pumpkin soup, a favorite of French slave masters. On Sunday, January 1, 1804, when they gained their freedom, they celebrated with music and food in the *Place d'Armes*, the [large plaza in the] city of Gonaives. And what better way to celebrate than to eat the very thing they were unable to eat as slaves? Nowadays it doesn't matter where in the world a Haitian might be on January 1—they will be having the soup of freedom."

117   **Mount Pelée:** Mount Pelée is an active volcanic mountain on the Caribbean island of Martinique located in the city of St. Pierre. When it erupted on May 8, 1902, about 30,000 of St. Pierre's residents died during the tragedy, including thirteen Spiritans. This is the largest number of casualties for a volcanic eruption in the twentieth century.

118	**John Chandler:** John Chandler was a great American traveler. When he arrived in Le Cap, he said that the city looked like St. Pierre in Martinique.

119	**Alexandre Dumas:** Born Dumas Davy de la Pailleterie (1802–1870) in Saint-Domingue, prolific French writer Alexandre Dumas was the grandson of Marie-Cessette Dumas, a black Haitian slave, and Alexandre Antoine Davy de la Pailleterie, an impoverished French nobleman. He is one of the most well-read French novelists whose works include *The Count of Monte Cristo*, *The Three Musketeers*, *Twenty Years After*, and *The Vicomte of Bragelonne: Ten Years Later*. He was called "the most Haitian of the French."

120	**Nord Alexis:** Pierre Nord Alexis (1820–1910) was President of Haiti from December 21, 1902 to December 2, 1908. Ousted from power, Alexis went into exile in Jamaica and later relocated to New Orleans, where he is buried in St. Louis Cemetery #2.

121	**Admiral Killick:** Admiral Hammerton Killick (1856–1902) was an Anglo-Haitian commander in the Haitian Navy. At the time of his death, Killick was aboard the La Crête-à-Pierrot, a newly acquired 940-ton screw gunship. Rather than surrender to German forces outside of Gonaïves, Haiti, Killick scuttled his own ship by igniting the magazine, and went down with his vessel. The main base for the Haitian Coast Guard, Killick, outside of Port-au-Prince is named for him. In 1943 he was additionally honored with a Haitian postage stamp bearing his image.

122	***L'intransigeant:*** *L'intransigeant* was a French newspaper that was vehemently anti-Dreyfusard. In 1906, it reached a circulation of 400,000 copies. It ceased publication after the French surrender in 1940. After the war, it was briefly republished in 1947 under the name *L'Intransigeant–Journal de Paris*, before merging with *Paris-Presse*.

123 **Edmond Rostand's** L'Aiglon: Edmond Eugène Alexis Rostand
(1868–1918) was a French poet and dramatist known best for his play
Cyrano de Bergerac. *L'Aiglon* is a play based on the life of Napoleon
II. The title of the play comes from a nickname for Napoleon II, the
French word for "eaglet." Sarah Bernhardt played the title role in
its premiere in March, 1900 at Théâtre Sarah Bernhardt. Rostand
had written *L'Aiglon* with Bernhardt in mind. It became one of her
signature roles.

124 **Latin:** Latin was taught at the St. Esprit Institution, alongside more
modern languages.

125 **Émile Combes:** Émile Justin Louis Combes (1835–1921) was a
French statesman and freemason who led the Right Block cabinet
in France between June 1902 and January 1905. His main policies
involved an anti-clerical agenda and the separation of church and
state in France. By 1904, through his efforts, nearly 10,000 religious
schools had been closed. In a letter, he ordered the teachers of the
Institution of St. Esprit to leave the premises. After the adoption of
the Law of Associations, the congregational schools were closing in
France, including the St. Esprit Institution.

126 **Baccalauréat:** The *baccalauréat* is an academic examination that
French students are required to take in order graduate high school.
Introduced by Napoleon I in 1808, it is the main diploma required to
pursue university studies. Similar university entrance qualifications
exist elsewhere in Europe. A senior at the Saint Esprit Institution,
Joseph Laroche had to take his *baccalauréat* and complete his high
school education. He passed with flying colors and attended his
graduation ceremony.

127 **Lille:** Joseph Laroche attended Faculté Catholique des Hautes
Études Industrielles in Lille, 150 kilometers from Beauvais. Lille is a
true college town—over 100,000 of its inhabitants are students. The
town is renowned for its summer markets, festivals and concerts.

One of its most notable events is the Braderie de Lille, the largest flea market in all of Europe, which takes place at the end of every summer. Café de Bellevue on the Grand Place, and Café Jean near the theater were Joseph Laroche's favorite hangout places in Lille.

128 **Louis Pasteur:** Louis Pasteur was a French chemist and microbiologist who made many important discoveries related to the immune system, vaccinations, chemistry and the nature of diseases. In 1848 he became professor of chemistry at the University of Strasbourg and in 1854 he became dean of the faculty of sciences at Lille University. A quote from Louis Pasteur: "I am utterly convinced that Science and Peace will triumph over Ignorance and War, that nations will eventually unite not to destroy but to edify, and that the future will belong to those who have done the most for the sake of suffering humanity."

129 **(The) Three Happy Days:** The Carnival of Dunkirk takes place from January to March where the crowds dress up to dance and parade in the streets. The culmination of the carnival takes place on the Three Happy Days—the Sunday, Monday and Tuesday preceding Ash Wednesday.

130 **Antoine Simon**: François C. Antoine Simon (1843–1923), also known as Antoine Simon, was president of Haiti from December 1908 to August 1911. He assumed the presidency after leading a successful coup d'état against Pierre Nord Alexis. Simon was in turn ousted in a coup d'état in 1911 led by General Cincinnatus Leconte. Leconte was a former Minister of Public Works and Agriculture who eventually replaced Simon as Haitian President. In *Tell My Horse*, Zora Neale Hurston describes an elaborate Catholic funeral Simon held for his pet goat, Simalo.

131 **Jamaica**: Jamaica is an island country situated in the Caribbean Sea. It is the third-largest island of the Greater Antilles and the fourth-largest island country in the Caribbean. Jamaica lies about

191 kilometers west of Hispaniola. Nord Alexis and Cincinnatus Leconte sought refuge in Jamaica after losing power in Haiti.

132   **Jean Victor Généus**: Jean Victor Généus is a Haitian Ambassador who wrote about historical relations between Haiti and Jamaica.

133   **L'Illustration:** *L'Illustration* was a French newspaper published in Paris from 1843 to 1944. In 1891, *L'Illustration* became the first French newspaper to publish a photograph. Many of these photographs came from syndicated photo-press agencies, but the publication also employed its own photographers. In 1907, *L'Illustration* was the first to publish a color photograph. It also published Gaston Leroux's novel *Le mystère de la chambre jaune* as a serial a year before its 1908 release. During Joseph Laroche's time in France, the newspaper reported on the inhumane conditions of the laborers who worked underground on the railroad.

134   *Le Matin***:** *Le Matin* is a daily newspaper published in Haiti founded on April 1, 1907.

135   **Cacos:** Cacos were groups of armed men, originally from the enslaved population of Haiti, who came to power in the mountainous regions of Haiti following the victory of the Haitian Revolution in 1804. The name "cacos" is derived from local terms for a bird, the red-plumed *Hispaniolan trogon* who hides in foliage. During the US occupation of Haiti in 1915, the Cacos maintained an armed rebellion against the US Marine Corps forces near Cap-Haïtien in the north. The Cacos eventually lost their rebellion and were destroyed at the battle of Fort Rivière in 1919. According to John J. Tierney Jr. on *The Institute of World Politics* website, "The Cacos had no military organization, no uniforms, no modern arm or supplies of their own, yet they fought the marines in guerrilla war from the first day of the intervention in 1915. They eventually lost, but not until 1922, not until they had succeeded in challenging the right of the US to govern Haiti itself, and not until their stubborn resistance had voiced its protests right up

to the halls of the US Congress and to the White House." Prominent Cacos leaders include Charlemagne Péralte and Benoît Batraville.

136   *Le Démocrate*: *Le Démocrate* was published every Saturday in Lecap, starting in 1876. Joseph's friend Luc Grimard worked for the newspaper.

137   **French fries:** Nobody can agree on where French Fries were invented, but supposedly they were used as a fish substitute back in the 1600s. The locals in Belgium would normally eat fried fish, but in the winter the river was frozen so they couldn't catch any fish. They turned to potatoes as a substitute. Today, almost one-fourth of all potatoes in America are consumed as French fries. In fact, Americans eat more than twenty-five pounds of French Fries every year. The largest serving of fries was served in Eagle, Idaho back in 2014—the fries weighed 1003 pounds.

138   **Buckwheat cake:** According to the website European Cuisines, "this traditional butter cake of the Breton region, almost a shortbread, is based on one of the staple grains of Brittany, buckwheat (called *blé noir* in French, or sometimes *farine de sarrasin*). Buckwheat frequently turns up as a major grain in places where there is little arable land to spare (mountainous regions usually) or places where the climate is too cool or wet to grow good wheat. It's a dense grain, lacking gluten, and so will never raise very high when used for baking: which is possibly why a much better-known baked product of Brittany is the famous but extremely flat Breton crêpe, the galette."

139   **Kate Buss:** Kate Buss (1875–1911) was a British Passenger on the *Titanic*. On the journey from Southampton to Queenstown she wrote a letter to her brother, Percy, using headed paper from the *Titanic*; in the letter, she mistakenly described Louise and Simone Laroche as Asian. She also described the beautiful music played by the *Titanic*'s orchestra.

140 **Les Dix Frères:** *Les Dix Frères* was a ship that endured a violent storm; one of the survivors related the events to Joseph.

141 **Father Thomas Byles:** Father Thomas Byles (1870–1912) was a British vicar on his way to New York to celebrate his brother's wedding. He died during the *Titanic*'s maiden voyage.

142 **Father Montvila:** Father Juozas Montvila (1885-1911) was born in Lithuania. In his time before boarding the *Titanic*, he administered Catholic rites in secrecy as practice of the Catholic faith was outlawed by the Russian Empire in Lithuania. Under government pressure, Fr. Montvila was forced to leave the country. He boarded the *Titanic* in Southampton, England, intending to continue his ministry in the US. Like the other priests aboard the *Titanic*, Fr. Montvila refused to evacuate, and reportedly fulfilled his priestly duties as the ship sank.

143 **Father Peruschitz:** Father Josef Peruschitz (Josip Perušić 1871–1911) was born Benedikt Peruschitz in Wolfratshausen, Bavaria. He taught mathematics, music, physical education, shorthand, and prefect conduct. Fr. Peruschitz boarded the *Titanic* in Southhampton. He had accepted a principal's position at the Swiss Congregation's Benedictine School in Minnesota. Unfortunately, he perished on board.

144 **Chicago (liner):** After the sinking of *Titanic* and her husband's death, Mrs. Laroche could not stand the thought of boarding a British vessel for another transatlantic journey, and instead chose the SS *Chicago*, a French Compagnie Générale Transatlantique liner. On May 1, 1912, Mrs. Laroche and her two daughters arrived safely in Le Havre, France, where her father awaited her return.

"I still think about the 'might have beens' about the *Titanic*, that's what stirs me more than anything else. Things that happened that wouldn't have happened if only one thing had gone better for her. If only, so many if onlys. If only she had enough lifeboats. If only the watertight compartments had been higher. If only she had paid attention to the ice that night. If only the Californian did come. The 'if only' kept coming up again and again and that makes the ship more than the experience of studying a disaster. It becomes a haunting experience to me, it's the haunting experience of 'if only.' "

—Walter Lord, *Titanic* historian and author

Mango Publishing, established in 2014, publishes an eclectic list of books by diverse authors—both new and established voices—on topics ranging from business, personal growth, women's empowerment, LGBTQ studies, health, and spirituality to history, popular culture, time management, decluttering, lifestyle, mental wellness, aging, and sustainable living. We were recently named 2019's #1 fastest growing independent publisher by *Publishers Weekly*. Our success is driven by our main goal, which is to publish high quality books that will entertain readers as well as make a positive difference in their lives.

Our readers are our most important resource; we value your input, suggestions, and ideas. We'd love to hear from you—after all, we are publishing books for you!

Please stay in touch with us and follow us at:

Facebook: Mango Publishing
Twitter: @MangoPublishing
Instagram: @MangoPublishing
LinkedIn: Mango Publishing
Pinterest: Mango Publishing

Sign up for our newsletter at www.mango.bz and receive a free book!

Join us on Mango's journey to reinvent publishing, one book at a time.

CPSIA information can be obtained
at www.ICGtesting.com
Printed in the USA
JSHW022002101221
21197JS00003B/3